REVIEW OF TWO WORLDS

REVIEW OF TWO WORLDS

French and American Poetry in Translation

]o[

Proceedings of the conference held April 4–6, 2003
at the Doheny Memorial Library,
University of Southern California

Edited by Béatrice Mousli

OTIS BOOKS /
SEISMICITY EDITIONS

A project of the Graduate Writing program
Otis College of Art + Design

LOS ANGELES • 2005

This publication was made possible by a grant from the French Cultural Services.

Book design, cover photograph, and typesetting: Guy Bennett

SEISMICITY EDITIONS
Graduate Writing program
Otis College of Art + Design
9045 Lincoln Boulevard
Los Angeles, CA 90045

http://gw.otis.edu/seismicity.html
seismicity@otis.edu

CONTENTS

Preface

The conference documented by the present volume grew out of the research and writing of Guy Bennett and Béatrice Mousli's *Charting the Here of There: French & American Poetry in Translation in Literary Magazines, 1850–2002,** a book which chronicles the on-going history of Franco-American literary exchanges. One of the untold stories of that history is that the poets themselves are chiefly responsible for it, often editing, translating, and publishing the poetry of their French or American colleagues in journals to which they either contribute or edit themselves. This being the case, we thought it would be enlightening to bring together a number of poets and translators currently involved in this exchange and ask them to share their views on the subject, discuss their practice, and read their work.

The encounter, which took place on April 4–6, 2003, was hosted by the Doheny Memorial Library of the University of Southern California, and the Graduate Writing Program of Otis College of Art + Design. Seventeen poets from both countries participated in four panels and three readings, all of which were open to the public. An exhibit was concurrently held in the Treasury Room of the Doheny Memorial Library, featuring French and American poetry journals from the mid-19th century through the present.† The exhibit was co-curated by Bennett, Mousli, and Tyson Gaskill, the library's Programming Director. Bi-lingual readings were given on both campuses as well as at Dawson's Book Shop.

* New York: Granary Books, 2002. A revised and expanded edition was published in French as: *Poésies des deux mondes. Un dialogue franco-américain à travers les revues 1850–2004.* Translated by Jean-Michel Espitallier & Marina Dick. Paris: Ent'revues, 2004.

† The exhibit *A Review of Two Worlds: French and American Poetry in Translation* ran from February 7–May 9, 2003.

We are indebted to many people and organizations without whose help neither the conference, the exhibit, nor this book would not have been possible. We would like to thank Tyson Gaskill, who personally oversaw every aspect of the conference and exhibit, the Cultural Services of the French Embassy in New York, the Florence Gould Foundation, and the Graduate Writing program at Otis College of Art + Design. We also thank Laurent Devèze, then Cultural Attaché of the French Consulate in Los Angeles, and his deputy, Antoine Châtelet, for their support and encouragement. Many thanks to Andrew Maxwell, who originally worked with us in preparing the conference and later left for new ventures. Last but not least, a very warm word of thanks to all of the poets and translators who accepted to join us in this adventure and whose work appears on the pages that follow.

Guy Bennett, Béatrice Mousli, & Paul Vangelisti

Panels & Papers

INFLUENCE & PERCEPTION

MATERIAL & CULTURAL SAMPLINGS

POLITICS, FORM & EXPERIMENT

TRANSLATING & (RE)SOURCE

Influence & Perception: Opening Remarks

BÉATRICE MOUSLI

One thing that quickly becomes apparent when you consider the recent literary histories of our two nations is the deep bond uniting French and American poetry over the last 150 years. What is not immediately apparent is why. Why is it, for example, that French and American poets are so frequently drawn to one another (much more so, it would seem, than to poets from other countries)? Why does this interest almost inevitably lead to translation? Why is this activity most evident in the area of "experimental" writing? In *Charting the Here of There,* we sought to respond to these questions first by studying the work of writers who over the years translated and published colleagues from the other country. We then questioned poets currently involved in the exchange, and asked them to tell us of their motivations and practices. We shall broaden that discussion here.

Eric Giraud tells of first encountering American poets while "rummaging and going through the shelves with a fine-tooth comb via *Origin Vort Angel Hair O-Blek Object Lesson* and *The Germ Chain Fence.*" He recalls reading American poetry "...in the beginning for the most part in French then in English." For Giraud the question of language is central to the encounter: he initially read translations, and later acquired a sufficient grasp of the foreign language to be able to understand the original. For Joseph Guglielmi it was "a complex attraction," a friendship so close that the other language wound up leaving an indelible mark on his own writing, which became "literally and figuratively" a "by-product of translation" as well as "a way of giving the French language a fuller shape and greater musicality."

For Douglas Messerli, language is not what first drew him to contemporary French poetry; rather it was the "common ground" he feels with it, finding it "very similar in its experimentation and energy to innovative American poetry." His view is shared by Cole Swensen, who believes it makes perfect sense that this exchange mainly takes place in the experimental community: "the French-American friendship is rooted in the revolutionary politics of the late 18th century and their common need to overthrow oppressive regimes." And she adds "revolutions are, by definition, experimental." She insists on the political nature of the relationship, and goes so far as to suggest that there is an "anarchical gesture, based in the friendship inherent in revolution."

Whatever their positions, the papers that follow all demonstrate how the perception of French poetry in America and American poetry in France is in fact shaped by the will and taste of individuals. By their very activity, translators, editors and publishers chart the geography of the general knowledge of foreign literatures, and readers will have to rely on their choices and trust their intuitions. Only time – and new *passeurs* – can fill out the blank spots on our old maps and/or provide new ones.

From One to The Other

JOSEPH GUGLIELMI

I won't really talk about fascination. But rather of a complex attraction on both sides, of tropisms that can vary from poet to poet. Depending on the circumstances of the discovery of the other language.

I will try not to generalize. And will limit myself to my own experience.

It is difficult for me to imagine a writer – whoever he may be – that knows only one language. The son of immigrants, I spent my childhood in the south of France, immersed in the Genovese dialect that my parents spoke, against a backdrop of Marseilles slang and the sounds – less important of course, but present nevertheless – of Corsican, which is still spoken by our neighbors. That is to say that early on I was aware, if unconsciously, of a kind of linguistic instability within a country and an educational system historically and officially marked by the spirit of a Jacobinian and multicultural France.

Moreover, my adolescence (1944) was strongly marked by the language of the liberators, the GIs, on whom I could try out the little English I had learned in two years of high school.

And let's not forget Jazz: its music and songs helped me maintain my interest in American English up to the 1970s, at which point I started to read and translate American poetry on a regular basis.

After a rather long *crise de vers*... which resulted in the book *Aube* that Rosmarie Waldrop translated so beautifully....

To read, to translate, *translater*, to use Valery Larbaud's expression, all share the same dynamism.

Everything came to me through friendship, on meeting Rosmarie and Keith Waldrop, Claude Royet-Journoud, Jacques Roubaud, and Mitsou Ronat in Paris. And around magazines, like *Action Poétique, Change*, as well as the anthology *20 Poètes Américains*, published by Gallimard in the late '80s, and for which Roubaud invited me to translate David Antin, Cid Corman, Larry Eigner, Jack Spicer, and Rosmarie Waldrop.

I went from readings to translations, and cannot forget those produced in the collective translation workshops at Royaumont. Royaumont is a place where poets from all over the world are welcomed and collectively translated. Regarding American poetry, I was able to translate David Antin, Norma Cole, Clark Coolidge, Jackson Mac Low, Craig Watson, among others, and to participate in panels with poets such as Michael Palmer, Michael Davidson, Michael Gizzi, Peter Gizzi, Stacy Doris, Chet Wiener, Serge Gavronsky, Rae Armantrout, Rosmarie Waldrop, Keith Waldrop, Carl Rakosi, Cole Swensen, Mei Mei Berssenbrughe, Rachel Blau Duplessis.... I also would like to mention the role played by the Biennale de Poésie du Val de Marne, organized by Henri Deluy, during which I have been able to speak with John Ashbery, Susan Howe, Jerome Rothenberg, whose *A Book of Witness* I have just translated with Tita Reut....

More or less all of these poets have marked my own writing, literally and figuratively. Those who read me have seen that fragments of English mixed with other languages are present in my poems. This is what Jacques Roubaud call "stuffing" and Anne-Marie Lilti "Multilingual poetry": "Modern and ancient languages are numerous.... Among them English is the most spoken."

I should add that the frequent traces of American English in my poetry are a by-product of translation, but they are also a way of giving the French language a fuller shape and greater musicality.

Experimental poetry? Can we really reduce the question to that expression? Moreover, it seems to me that the new generation of French poets do not feel the same attraction, the same fascination, for American poetry. I think that the relationship between the two poetries is more complex than it seems. Poets like Anne-Marie Albiach, Michel Couturier, Roubaud, Deguy, Royet-Journoud, Tita Reut, and Emmanuel Hocquard, to mention but a few, have each perceived this phenomenon in their own way, and there is no real consensus. Other writers like Yves di Manno, Serge Fauchereau, Denis Roche, whom we should not forget, Jacques Darras, Jean Daive, Bernard

Noël, Dominique Fourcade, Jean-Jacques Viton, Pierre Alferi, Denis Dormoy, or Philippe Mikriammos (with whom I translated Coolidge), Paol Keineg.... And there are others ... are all excellent translators and all have different – even contradictory – views on American poetry.

For me, it was the *Cantos* that – and it is so common to say this – opened the door to this huge and contradictory domain. At the same time, in the sixties, I discovered Dylan Thomas, the Welsh poet who became famous in the U.S.

Later, it was Larry Eigner, Jerry Rothenberg, Jack Spicer, and even Joyce with *Finnegan's Wake* that inspired, to stick with English, my book *La Préparation des titres*.

With Ezra Pound, it was the Objectivists, and especially Zukofsky and Oppen that brought me to a new "reading" of the quotidian, while a writer like Burroughs broke down sexual taboos, a question avoided by most French poets at the time.... In the same area, and taking their differences into account, I met Kathy Acker, who died too young, and whose fiery work I truly appreciated....

I am tempted to believe that the "importance" of poetry is equaled only by its diversity. And the link between the two phenomena is created essentially by translation.

I think that American poetry brought some freedom to French poetry, which had long been pompous, and threatened by two dangers: on the one hand by its poetic-realistic-socialist engagement, and on the other, by the imitation of Surrealism.... But that's all in the past. Today, the very newest French poetry faces other dangers that I will not go into here.

And there is one text that we have not yet mentioned: Charles Olson's *Projective Verse*. There should be a complete study of this essay, which I am unfortunately not able to do. Charles Olson leads us to the Black Mountain College, that ultra-free university and temple of poetry and the arts which he lead with John Cage, Robert Duncan and Robert Creeley. In addition to Olson, there are other names that have marked American poetry for the last three decades. Names that I drop, knowing how fully biased I am, after big wigs William Carlos Williams, Cummings, Pound, Lorine Niedecker and the Beats, whom we should not forget because they inspired French poets like Pélieu, Heidsieck, Lebel, Blaine....

They are, from East to West, John Ashbery, Bob Creeley, Frank O'Hara, Larry Eigner, Jack Spicer, Michael Palmer, Jerry Rothenberg, Robert Duncan.... Names that always come to the mind of those who like American poetry, which is as lively as ever. They are also the names of wonderful readers of poetry....

We should also mention the closely knit network of small presses which covers the U.S., and the holy places of poetry readings, like the Poetry Project at Saint Mark's Church in the Village....

Let's open the circle. We meet Lou Reed, Bukowski, Leonard Cohen in Canada....

No set theory, but a fascinating nebula flashing with those names that come to my memory, to my mind, according to the randomness of encounters, the elusive rhythm of life....

I know I left out the younger generation of American poets. I did not say a word about the LANGUAGE poets, of the excellent Charles Bernstein, whom I met in Royaumont with Lyn Hejinian, of Craig Watson whom I translated....

A good way to keep up with all of it is to read the Format Américain chapbook series, created by Juliette Valéry and Emmanuel Hocquard, and *last but not least*, to reread the magazines *Banana Split*, *If*, *Java*....

There are still so many things to say.... You can always ask me questions!

And to conclude that which does not have a conclusion, here is a fragment by John Ashbery; to my mind, it is a good summary of the situation:

> My, we have raced to be equivocally here and have invented what sign? Off of what do we climb to the lower level, what compact fleet of stairs is nestled here? Or did we bowdlerize each other's delirium in fear of having the last word, and it frightened us off the page? In any case have a ripping good time. The boars will be here around then, as you know.

Post scriptum

It is no longer necessary to prove the importance, the influence of poets like T.S. Eliot and Gertrude Stein. I mention them because to me they seem to represent two antagonistic movements. The first was still a traditional lyricism. The second opened the way for what we could call a more impersonal poetry.... But if we take a closer look and, as far as I am concerned, after some scraping, I really discovered Eliot in an English-Italian bilingual edition, so I have a more musical and rhythmic impression of this poet, far from French, and precise meaning (of signified, if you like)....

◦ *Translated by Béatrice Mousli*

Investigative Poetics / Investigative Politics

COLE SWENSEN

Why does the mutual interest among French and American poets appear mostly in the experimental community? Because the French-American friendship is rooted in the revolutionary politics of the late 18th century and their common need to overthrow oppressive regimes. And revolutions are, by definition, experimental. They depend upon the willingness of every "party" in sight to experiment wildly.

That's just an idea. The question is one I've been considering for years, and I often come up with ideas, but never really an answer. And I only air this current lack-of-an-answer because the question touches on such important issues, which current events have made excruciatingly present.

Could we broaden the question: "Why do experimental poetics and multi-language activities go hand in hand?" I'd like to say yes, but that's a little idealistic; conservative translators and translations are all too numerous. Yet experimentalism and multi-lingualism often do go hand-in-hand in contemporary French-American exchanges, and there is, even now, a political dimension to the experimentalism they share.

To leave your language is to leave your nation and/or to expand your language is to expand your nation – just a slight rephrasing of Wittgenstein's well-known, "The limits of my language are the limits of my world." To narrow that down to the discussion at hand: there's a correlation between investigative poetics and investigative social practices.

Could we substitute *progressive* for *investigative* in both instances? And then, of course, how would we be defining *progress*? Despite these mares' nests, a large majority of experimental poets (and frankly, of poets *period*) in the U.S. and Europe are leftists strongly opposed to the current war.

Historically – with some monumental exceptions, such as Marinetti,

Pound, and Eliot – leftist politics and experimental poetics have a history of constructive companionship. I don't want to suggest a connection between conservative poetics and nationalism as much as its correlate: a connection between experimental poetics and internationalism.

And not even an internationalism so much as an "a-nationalism" – for while politics are very much at the core of artistic experimentation, the term "internationalism" still supports the concept of nationhood, which supports just the sort of arbitrary, divisive, and constrictive boundaries that innovative poetries work to erode in language and aesthetics, and thus also in thought and belief.

Translation operates at a confluence of abandonments – right where the nation abandons its boundaries, just as the self, in going beyond its own language, abandons its self. Translation does this by attacking the name, the most binding, constricting function in language. Translation is anonymous, and it spawns anonymities. It thwarts the ownership of a given text and of language at large through multiplication and proliferation. It erases the name both of the author and his or her country by overflowing each; it annihilates through abundance. It is distinctly post-deluvian.

But this doesn't answer the questions "why France and America?" and "why the experimental?"

The experimental tradition that informs much contemporary American work began in France – Aloysius Bertrand invented the prose poem; Baudelaire recast the poles of the beautiful and the ugly; Rimbaud redrafted subjectivity; Mallarmé redefined the page. On the other hand, other principal instigation to literary modernism came from America, with Whitman's renovated line and Poe's insight into the altered nature of urban subjectivity. Modernist experimentation arose seemingly separately but contemporaneously in both languages, with a somewhat uneven but mutual recognition, which is traced in the *Charting* book.

As that book also mentions, between the wars, Americans were driven to France by "the enforced Puritan attitude that characterized the American scene." That attitude has never fundamentally changed – having dug in its heels before the country was even founded, it remains one of those constraints so deeply embedded in American daily life that no American

can possibly remain constantly conscious of it. It's too pervasive; it's an integral part of the ambient lighting, operating as a limit in just the way that a habitual, unexamined use of language does.

The person resistant to the one will also likely be resistant to the other. And may, either consciously or unconsciously, attempt to address constrictive social practices by operating upon the more readily available, more tangible parallel of language – a displacement that's both accurate and effective, as those social practices always need language as their most basic collaborator.

The puritanical, the self-righteously restrictive, brings us back to the question of the connection of nationalism to aesthetic conservatism. This has many precedents – socialist realism in support of the Soviet State; Hitler's refusal of "decadent" art, and in the U.S., Norman Rockwell, Grant Wood, the compromised NEA. Throughout the 20th century, American artists and writers have been refusing such limitations simply by leaving the country, with the most experimental often going to France. Again, it's well-documented in the book *Charting*. As is the reverse trend – most notably, the wave of writers and artists who came to New York during World War II. And it is a wave; it goes back and forth, depending on the political climate, but always operating below the formal political horizon. It's always an anarchical gesture, based in the friendship inherent in revolution, whether those past or in the future.

The Making

ERIC GIRAUD

There's something to be told about us for the telling of which we all wait according to Laura Riding it's the only sentence that I'm leaving in English as I begin again this written communication to be read today in Los Angeles this fascination between France and America and vice versa is not clear we would need a sociologist as well as a historian in order to figure it out in any case I do not know too much about it so I apply myself to do the magazines the time taken the produced energy the created objects the worked texts the magazines where I have read American poets it was in the beginning for the most part in French then in English and we will see why Eugene Jolas's magazine *Transition* where there is a text by Bob Brown the typography and the page-setting of the covers and the multilingualism of texts if memory serves because I have no sample here where I write this morning of September 29, 2003 just two days before the deadline to turn it in for publication just at the center of the room there are some issues and then *Commerce Fontaine L'Arbalète Perspectives* which is called *Profils* in French this multilingual magazine established in several countries where the texts concerning the United States are often more interesting than the poems or the fiction published *Change* with all these poems by Spicer translated by Jacques Roubaud *Les Lettres Nouvelles Zuk Banana Split* and *la Revue de Littérature Générale* as well as *Action Poétique* where I read the translation of *Lifting Belly If* where Holly Dye and I translated our first poems and thereafter a lot of American poetry but also *Java* and some others I have forgotten involuntarily voluntarily it was necessary before that to research and conduct a little survey of anthologies first to find a way in the work of those who are already working in this field in the years since that task in these anthologies or special issues of magazines compiled by Serge Fauchereau

Jacques Roubaud Michel Deguy Claude Royet-Journoud Emmanuel Hocquard and Jean-Jacques Viton and leave with reading the foreign language of poetry I sought after a few years of reading in French to force the foreign in reading foreign languages in a foreign language there was nothing more adventurous than to find yourself in front of your own language after a few years of reading it happened to me to better read in translating than in reading sometimes that's why in translating what we were asked to translate first then in rummaging and going through the shelves with a fine-tooth comb via *Origin Vort Angel Hair O-blek Object Lesson* then *The Germ Chain Fence* I found from time to time texts to translate manners of thinking with the language of people to meet but there were also the visits to used bookstores in San Francisco Berkeley New York Portland which during our fairly long stay in the United States first a way to kill time gave me something to do and discovering little by little on its shelves all the bargains and rare or used books like those that one sees everywhere in twenty five thousand copies or those which no one ever talks about again or have never talked about that lasting thousands of hours where I was still learning to discover the ones I didn't yet know but to revisit at the beginning some texts some books struck a blow to my head to my face in my heart all at the same time and first the translation of Jack Spicer's *Billy the Kid* by Joe Gugliemi in this little yellow edition in large format the translation of John Taggert's *Poème de la Chapelle Rothko* by Pierre Alferi and Emmanuel Hocquard in this little dark red edition in large format the translation of *Lifting Belly* by Alix C. Roubaud and Jacques Roubaud Charles Reznikoff's poems for the magazine *If* Charles Olson's for the Théâtre Typographique that were translated with Holly Dye or Crush this little text by Lee Ann Brown translated for Juliette Valery's collection of chapbooks where I discovered poets like Juliana Sphar Jena Osman Bill Luoma Julie Kalendek but I remember now that meanwhile I had done quite a bit of research in order to invite some poets working on the connection between poetry and film in order to organize meetings in Marseilles around poetry and American film aided at that time by the inexhaustible collection of undubbed American poetry started from a generous donation from Jacques Roubaud where rather than sell it for practically nothing because of moving house he no longer had space in the exiguity of Parisian real estate for this voluminous collection which we had started to put in order with Olivier Devers that then I have year after year modestly augmented by a few purchases and by gifts especially from poets and that's how we translated for the journal for this event Peter Gizzi Lee Ann Brown Jalal Toufic and still others with whom we kept in touch some of them including Peter with whom a true work of connection was transformed and changed into a true friendship and it is by reading a poem by John Yau that I discovered Laura Riding's *Telling* her language first in the process of reasoning of the search for the idea in the work of the language but not necessarily the sense of the world or of life that she seems to desire at all costs and that interests us a little less yes there are poems that remain in one's head for a long time because we have translated them a long time the best of the readings could be a remark and the second in disorder saying that the translation starts with the choice of the poem of the passage of the text of the book to translate and especially what one gets from and takes of the poet's language what one learns and introduces into one's own writing far from looting it is a more profound borrowing that greatly enriches the language of the translating author who wants still to be open and growing here are several oblique and indirect responses it's like that which we wanted to also reexamine that which Stein says of the questions in the 924 (?) pages of the making of the Americans then I worked with Eric Pesty opposite me in this office he had just arrived and started to be interested in American poetry to join me in this interest from there it came to us in Marseille behind our desks that face each other the idea of a magazine then of the name of this magazine driving one day in the direction of Half Moon Bay in a curve « I*s*sue » with one italic and one regular facing each other to move the field of the magazine of the creation to foreign terrain and in foreign language was maybe the only way to make a magazine of poetry of creation that did not resemble all of the others later I was going to forget it was added D. Lespiau who produced the final design for the magazine and accelerated things for the printing and the idea was always to really add something and to use the translation as a base of departure even if it means to make it or to bypass it to divert it or just to outline it starting from the translation we could perhaps get to something else at a search for writing at a formation of another language of slightly new forms here are our unmethodical interrogations just like the field the vast field just like the man's land of America are not initially an obsession an *americanomania* an *americanophagia* but a place a place of displacement a space full open and empty at the same time a space distant enough for a better overview or a better work table and the good idea if ever we had any was to make only a definite number in advance of issues five issues only then all to stop and be able thus to work a little better on the concept of series of combination of assembly since an issue being a series of texts a magazine of issues being also a series of issues as if these five issues at the end of the year 2004 made of it nothing more than a series of series an assembly the work of a form here it always remains something to be told something to be told for the telling of which we all work.

◦ *Translated by Melinda Menjou*

Remarks on Influence & Perception

DOUGLAS MESSERLI

Cole, you brought up some very interesting perceptions in your discussion. However, I'm not sure that all – or even most – American poets do feel a sense of liberation with regard to French poetry and culture; nor do they even care about "the liberation" we feel very strongly about. I'm going to begin with a vast generalization, which admitedly is an overstatement, but I think useful in discussing the American interest – or I should say, the American experimental poet's interest in – French poetry and literature in general. Namely, American culture tends to fall on either of two sides of European influence, sides divided in actual terms by the English Channel.

I'd say the great majority of American poets and critics would characterize themselves as "Anglophiles," that is people whose primary literary influence – if there is an outside influence – is from England. Certainly, this would characterize most university and college-based poets writing in what we might describe as the more "traditional" forms of poetry. These poets, aligned with T.S. Eliot, would see themselves as belonging to a long tradition of English poets, from the 18th century down through the 20th century with figures such as Yeats, Hardy, Spender, Plath (who I'm going to characterize against the reality as English), Hughes, and some contemporary figures. In nonpoetic expression we can see this most clearly in the kind of Merchant-Ivory productions of British novels – Forster, Woolf, etc. Many Americans, and I might almost say, "most" Americans eat this up. They adore all the comfy charm of the English countryside and that sort of careful expression of moral gratitude so clearly expressed in both the fiction and poetry of England.

Then there are the rest of us – primarily innovative in our activities – who might describe ourselves as Francophiles. We need only to look to the great tradition of modern French poetry – beginning with Rimbaud and Apollinaire, and moving straight through the century in the expressions of Jarry, Jacob, Ponge, Jabès, Breton, and Valéry, and encompassing the Fracophone traditions of Césaire, Dib and others – to recognize our roots or, at least, a common ground. I think, in this context, we find contemporary French poetry to be very similar in its experimentation and energy to innovative American poetry, beginning with the New York School and extending to "Language" poetry and beyond.

I do think it is important, moreover, to recognize that Americans sit on both sides of the fence so to speak. It would be smug of us, I believe, to presume that most Americans quickly recognize France as a poetic ally – or, in the case of contemporary politics – even a political ally. Those of us who do look to France see things very differently from those in the U.S. who don't perceive this. Marjorie Perloff, in her essay "Avant Garde Eliot," makes this difference quite apparent in her discussion of Eliot's transformation from a young "avant-garde" poet very much in love with France (and befriended by Jean Verdenal) into the later self-conciously British poet of *Four Quartets*. Like many of the differences between British and French culture, the two American poetic traditions are not always compatible, and, I believe, might help to explain why there are such waring factions in American poetry.

Obviously, one could find as many exceptions to what I have just outlined as they could find examples, but I think that when we say there is a major American-French connection we have to recognize some delimitations.

Having begun there, I think we can now go back over some of what Cole Swensen has argued for, that France has long represented to many Americans a country and a culture that allows for the liberation that American culture did not/and *will not* always allow. Certainly for the generation after World War I, Paris was a life-saver, a place where one could be free to write and experiment, and drink – yes that too was important – and play and participate in the adventure of a more liberated way of being. As Béatrice pointed out in the discussion after the delivery of this paper, however, that did not mean that the Americans in Paris were directly in contact with French authors. Indeed they treated Paris very much like an American suburb, and very seldom met with or even communicated with French literary figures.

I find that very disturbing, because I do feel today that many American poets, several of them sitting in this very room, do have close connections with writers such as Jacques Roubaud, Emmanuel Hocquard, Joe Guglielmi, Dominique Fourcade, Jean Frémon, Henri Deluy, Olivier Cadiot, and numerous others. And that has been a fruitful relationship that has stimulated and, in part, transformed American poetics.

Moreover, as a publisher, I have found it truly exciting to be able to publish the works of many of these important authors. It has meant that I have been able to make much of the French poetic scene available for American poets who might seldom get to France, and have no real contact with French writers themselves.

I will not say, however, that the relationship of which I speak has been unilateral. I think French translators and publishers work very differently from American translators and publishers. Our tendency here is to read a large body of work and translate that work which we feel has the highest merit. In France, on the other hand, it appears that actual contact with Americans is necessary before publication; and, in particular, it seems that if one speaks French then one is more likely to be represented in French translation. As Eric Giraud makes clear in his comments of how he has come to read American figures, the choices are often personal and accidental; and this, in turn, seems to have left French literature with some very large misunderstandings or just laspses of knowledge about the American poetic scene. While I certainly see the value of approaching the poetry of a different culture in a very personal manner, it would be more helpful, I believe, if those French translators and poets who are fluent in English, would present others in France with a wider range of American poetry.

But this is only to quibble about a relationship which we all feel wonderful about, and are here today to celebrate!

Panels & Papers

INFLUENCE & PERCEPTION

MATERIAL & CULTURAL SAMPLINGS

POLITICS, FORM & EXPERIMENT

TRANSLATING & (RE)SOURCE

Introduction to the Panel: Material & Cultural Samplings

]o[

BÉATRICE MOUSLI

*What is the role/history of appropriation and collage in your practice of literature? To what extent are material and cultural samplings relevant to your own writing?** Such were the questions put to the members of this panel. Their responses could not have been more different: while Michel Bulteau describes himself as the heir of a long line of writers, Stacy Doris created a piece written using sampling and cut-up techniques, and Christophe Fiat outlines his theory for a new writerly aesthetic using sound as its base.

To illustrate what he sees as the base of the mechanics of creation, an "emotional pillage" as he puts it, Bulteau goes back to the works of Charles Nodier, Lautréamont, and Claude Pélieu. The 19th-century Nodier is described as the "master of the art of *détournement,* appropriation, and collage," while Lautréamont is presented as the champion of re-appropriation, the borrower. Closer to us, friend and translator of William Burroughs, Bob Kaufmann, Allen Ginsberg and others, Claude Pélieu did much to introduce the cut-up method in France, and was thus very influential on the younger generation. Inspired by the American poets and their poet-translator, Bulteau developed his own take on their tradition, *la méthode-pliage,* another form of appropriation, "a new creative process" aiming at "the control of discontinuity."

Quoting other sources – Felix Guattari, Gilles Deleuze, and Jacques Derrida – Christophe Fiat goes further in the exploration of new techniques, introducing sound and developing the concept of an "audio-literature,"

* This panel was chaired by Andrew Maxwell, who did not provide a written introduction for this publication.

where music, dance, writing, and voice come together in a "sampler," transforming the book into an ULO – an Unknown Literary Object – with a new aesthetic governed by the notion of "fun." This new type of literature is no longer "anxious about its destiny as language, nor . . . racked by the notion that its thoughts are somehow alienated through being transcribed in the book"; rather it is a literature that has found "a final but renewable mode of existence."

Putting the concept into practice, Stacy Doris considers her use of sampling while admiring a ceramic pony she was given during the conference and watching TV news late at night, thus creating a piece that illustrates her notions of time, art, and friendship as she reminds herself that "borrowings may influence form to the same extent that form may determine borrowings."

Some Examples of Détournement, *Appropriation, & Collage in French Literature*

MICHEL BULTEAU

The pursuit of words is a merciless one. I've never held the belief that the real is given up *immediately* to the mind. Rather, the real must be conquered. This conquest is the artist's work.

We may note then that the conquest of the inner life of things is necessarily a sort of plunder. Writing consists of besieging the real belonging to us all. Oscar Wilde said that life and literature constitute the two highest arts. Passing from one to the other seems to me profoundly immoral. The infinitesimal life of the poet is hugely immoral. This transgression has no precise application, save perhaps to deprive a word of its ordinary meaning.

Mind and matter are at cross-purposes. The pursuit of words, sensations, and images unfolds in the territory that divides them. The artist creates nothing all of a piece. It is an emotional pillage where one does not hesitate to ransack or help oneself to the endless spoils already amassed by other artists come before.

It'll have been necessary for the poet, in the first phase of this relentless pursuit, to have clear sight: in eyes and spirit both. But what'll bring the booty to light, if I may dare say so, will be the turn to music, to the mastery of verse and prose, or what Wilde called "true rhythmic life or words"….

Let's then turn ourselves now to three French writers who were themselves masters of the art of *détournement*, appropriation, and collage.

CHARLES NODIER: SCHOLAR, HOAXER

In a difficult-to-acquire work, Charles Nodier, the delightful author of *Smarra, or Demons of the Night,* deals with the subjects of imitation, literary theft and subject interpolation, etc....

Nodier is a scholarly hoaxer and a virtuoso of deception. In a curiously volatile and musical book (where all the chapter titles end in "tion") we read that "the first book written was itself not only a pastiche of tradition, but a plagiarism of the spoken word!"

What is certain is that Nodier is not an imitator without conscience. An admirable conductor, he is capable of inserting the most unexpected collages into his score, worrying little over chronology or related sensibility. He considers himself as the editor of the work of "the most tireless arranger of the period." Was he speaking, in fact, of one of his masters: Sterne?

Closer to home, a collection written (or rewritten) by Charles Nodier comes to light in 1822. This is *Infernalia*, a sort of fantastic, extravagant symphony in thirty movements. By the author's own confession, for the construction of this anthology he'd have borrowed from numerous different authors; at least five movements from Don Augustin Calmet; from Father Nicolas Langlet-Dufresnois, perhaps four movements. As for *Aventures de Thibaud de la Jacquière,* (as we know from Nodier's handwritten manuscript) we find their source in the tenth day of Jean Potocki's *Manuscrit trouvé à Saragosse* (translated in the U.S. as *Tales from the Saragossa Manuscript*).

Nodier had always been interested in the problem of dreams....

In a short account, *L'amour et le grimoire,* Nodier confesses: "One of the great childish passion I've known in my life is the desire to find myself among the heroes of fantasy, among the heroes of a fantastic story...."

And well, with *Infernalia*, it's a done deal.

RATIONAL PLUNDER IN LAUTRÉAMONT

In Lautréamont's writing, the momentum says a lot. We can think of this momentum like the great gaping mouth of a god that must be fed incessantly. *Les Chants de Maldoror*, a poem of fiery flows, a poem of a primitive ambiguity struggling toward a resolution of contrary parts, has necessarily borrowed a bit, if not badly, to sustain the strong force of its combustion. The rational plunder of Lautréamont is brilliant and effective. We know there was much borrowed from the Divine Comedy, from Byron and even Lamartine. But perhaps the least hidden appropriation are those taken from scientific publications like *Le Magasin pittoresque*, dedicated to seabird hunting, like that seen in the first Song of the book. The most famous collage concerns the flight of starlings, toward the beginning of the fifth Song. Lautréamont elsewhere clarifies: "Without a doubt, between the two extreme types of literature, that which you are used to [he is speaking here to the reader], and my own, there are infinite things between and it would be easy to multiply the divisions...."

An article appeared in 1952 in *Mercure de France* that demonstrated that Lautréamont had largely borrowed, sometimes even out of whole cloth from the *Encyclopédie d'histoire naturelle* (1850–1851) of Doctor Chenu, which inspires the descriptions made by Buffon and his collaborator Guéneau de Montbelliart. Charles Nodier similarly maintained that Buffon's *Histoire des Oiseaux* "is nearly all the work of Guéneau."

Lautréamont, in this delicate operation or reappropriation, remains a consummate master thief....

CLAUDE PÉLIEU AND THE CUT-UP

Brion Gysin, American painter and writer, who lived in Tangiers and Paris, employed what he called "the cut-up method," allowing writers the very collage technique that painters and visual artists had been using for fifty years. "The pages of a text are cut up and rearranged and form new combinations of words and images," writes William S. Burroughs, a fan of the technique.

The Franco-American poet Claude Pélieu (1934–2002), translator, among others, of Ginsberg, Kaufman and Burroughs, had also been one to use the cut-up method. In exile in the United States from 1963 on, he was a confidant of Burroughs. Their correspondence and the texts that they wrote together remain to be explored and are a testament to the power of this literary technique.

In 1969 Claude Pélieu published *Ce que dit la bouche d'ombre dans le bronze étoile d'une tête*, subtitled "new cut-up," which marvelously illustrates these violent *decoupages* and the bold reinsertions of his own work (holding thus to that axiom held dear to Burroughs: "I am a living cut-up").

AN EXPERIENCE TAKEN TO THE EXTREME

In my personal work, I have also been tempted by those "points of intersection" that Burroughs speaks about. In effect the literary methods proposed by Gysin in the Sixties and developed by the author of *Nova Express* were a liberating breath of fresh air. It was much more than a simple hovering and dust-up. The writers had begun to understand again that words know best their proper place. Living words. Like animals, they do not like to be bound (by the book).

Rather than the cut-up, I have experimented with "la méthode Pliage" (the fold-in method). Four texts belonging to the collection "Coquillarge – Rétroviseur" resume by extension the cut-up method. They are the four "poems" that compose the second part of the book.

The experience is pushed to the extreme and the reading of them consequently is likewise. Read, for example, the beginning of the fourth text:

> "qui sand froid G très chaud, L'avanantes d'enfants
> percore plus encombrées, un grand blonriane, lui-même de
> de bleu – Shelley sur la mort: immobmort, il dort parmi
> pour crier...."

The translation of these lines is naturally impossible.

I remember having folded up some articles appearing in magazines for teenagers. These articles relate the concert given in Hyde Park by the Rolling Stones in homage to Brian Jones. I have no memory of "readjusting" or "rearranging" the result of these various folds. No personal text was interposed there, so the resulting ensemble is not terribly comprehensible, but rather baffling.

It's necessary to remind oneself of something Burroughs said: "I'd like to insist on the fact that the fold-in method is a technique, and like any technique it can benefit some writers and act as a disservice to others – in this way it is an experimental situation – it's not an argument."

I quickly understood this. The world Burroughs gives us, sometimes by these methods (cut-up, fold-in), is not merely the result of these methods. Each writer is the *proprietor* of his or her own psychological and literary rhythm. If he or she is separate from others, he or she is still in communion with the world at large. The writer is not a weak person in the service of stronger persons. Before prosecutors and judges, the writer displays his or her singularity.

Is literary appropriation really a matter of transgression, of crossing a forbidden threshold? I'm not certain. This act is only, in sum, the first step in a new creative process that ultimately envisions, at its end, the control of discontinuity.

The master thief never forgets to take an account. That part of the road ignored by others is the one he quickly moves to call his own, like a child adding additional tracks to her electric train. It's a way of finding a perfect moment that felicitous feeling of rescue. Discovery saves us.

◦ *Translated by Andrew Maxwell*

Ceramic Ponies: Sampling a Paper on Borrowing

STACY DORIS

Shakespeare sampled Plutarch. Melville sampled Israel Potter. John Coltrane did not sample Rodgers and Hammerstein; that was something else. Borrowing has a prosody and a syntax which is in each case formally precise and exacting, yet in each case different and largely undocumented. At least sampling mostly asks if you believe it; can you believe that. Whereas sampling is a kind of pure documentation turned back on itself. Syntax. Jimi Hendrix did not sample "The Star Spangled Banner," he critiqued its nationhood. I was invited to participate on Andrew Maxwell's panel on sampling, cultural appropriation and inter-genre work in French and English. Jen Hofer and Melissa Dine, they live there if only sampling could be critical by dint of its repetitions – if only poetry could. Borrowings may influence form to the same extent that form may determine borrowings. They invite me to stay with them but I have to stay at the Furama Hotel to be near where the panel is to be. In each successful case, a new language is created from a multiplicity of languages and idiolects. So they lend me a ceramic pony which was a gift from them to their friend who had left it at their house for safe keeping. The idea is for the pony, which had a slot for money use of technology is not new – and borrowing from a range of technologies has always made sense in terms of writing being a primary technology itself to make me feel more at home, but on condition that I carry it everywhere around with me. Whenever I am in the hotel room the American invasion of Iraq is on TV. Americans claim they have taken Baghdad + video to prove it certain Iraqi sources say that is footage of a town outside Baghdad; Americans lie; Sadaam Hussein is walking around Baghdad fans cheering him certain U.S. sources say that is not Hussein is dead, that is footage of a Sadaam look-alike because these techniques are part of the tradition of poetry in perhaps all cultures; I am not acquainted with all of them. But if you take just as a random example, the traditional bard from ancient Greece or present day West Africa all the while, at the same time, over and over. You might say that techniques of appropriation are poetry's consciousness, in a sense of a socio-political awareness and the way poetic language interacts with the cultures at hand a girl Jessica Lynch is unconscious I see as part of the inherently investigative apparatus of poetry. I would say that such techniques are useful in allowing us to a hospital in Germany and we know what she will eat for breakfast when the coma is over, and there are many details about what is not known to have happened to her before she ended up this way that in France and the U.S. at present the number of publishing and emerging poets working along these lines would at least equal if not outnumber those who don't, and I also think that these practices are present in what you might consider 'investigative' poetries and in what you might not consider investigative ones. Haleh Hatami who does the same thing with Kerbala Redux sampling a Reuters report on the downed Apache helicopter and a Taziyeh script so what, Kate Pringle whose work in progress reminds me of how Walter Benjamin the latest blow in the propaganda war," Iraqi television showed what it called a near the city of Kerbala, 70 miles southwest of Baghdad. I am the calamity of Kerbala. Iraqis waving rifles reportedly danced around the black ,which appeared intact. The U.S. military confirmed that one of its helicopters had gone down, but so far refuses to comment on Iraqi claims that a second helicopter was shot down by "brave peasants." I have not seen in these wretched times any better than my own beloved supporters. The pilots are reportedly being held captive. On this transitory earth, no man is ever immortal. Britain and the U.S. have condemned the showing of pictures of Iraqi forces humiliating POWs wanted to set up some sort of text where citations could correspond with each other like conversing; which is what Norma Cole really I saw her do it the year before what is the difference between citation and sampling so if I sample myself am I sampling Pierre Joris brought up how most poetry like 99% of it in the world today is oral, that must be, Jean-René Etienne brought up *doujinshi*. Fan-comics, although some professional *mangakas* (manga writers) do *doujinshis* of their own work and although what we commonly associate with fan activities (fan-fiction for example) tends to be very misleading. Because *doujinshi* is not sloppy. It can be, but it can also be better that the original. The other defining feature is self-publishing. A doujinshi has to be self-published. Or community-published. After which my class on African American songs recorded in the South before World War II starts trying *doujinshi,* and Jean-René became can we translate a genre, can we call translation a genre If so it is perhaps a genre that is inherently inter – ts use of appropriation overt. Creating a language that falls between languages it examines by its very nature distances and circumscriptions among poets and socio-political practices. But all poetry does that. And yet not to the extent that we might hope. With Robert Kocik and others I have often discussed the role of poets as moving among disciplines, exposing science for scientists politics for the politicians. Taking concepts and language from these fields of inquiry, and reflecting them back in ways that point to possibilities the discipline did not know it had. Reenvisioning cultural practices to locate their positive creative potential. But not I am not so sure about all that. Not right this extended minute. I got a new computer and transferred all my files thousands of files from the old ones to the new one. In June I was walking just along the border of the parvis of the Beaubourg and there was Béatrice calling down to me from the balcony of a cocktail party at the *Quinzaine Littéraire,* even though I would tell Binky later that evening that I never run into people I know on the street in Paris. So I went up to say hi and Béatrice told me I would have to send her the text of my paper by October but I didn't listen. Because I'd lost the text of my paper, I didn't have a paper, remember, I had the borrowed ceramic pony. I don't need my paper anymore, the pony's my interface I wing the presentation. I say one thing that people seemed to like, something about how we are all samples, made up of a mix of mixtures but you have to be there obviously. In May, on my birthday, except I couldn't walk, Jen and Melissa came to Berkeley and borrowed me from my own poetry reading to give me the present of a ceramic pony from the same mold but not the same one which still belonged to their friends, but a pink one. I lent it to Kate Pringle's girlfriend who said she wanted to make the pink pony a movie star. Kate says she takes it everywhere and films it. This is a good life for a borrowed ceramic horse of any color. Now out of rancor I shall plunder your garden, I shall cause your cries to reach the heavens by my cruelty. U.S. President George Bush also shied from setting a timetable, saying it will last "however long it takes" to win. It is time I make haste, *Enshallah,* stirrup the foot of high purpose, *Enshallah* Well but I was able to dig up a kind of very preliminary draft of working notes for what I would have done had that horse never come along.

Under What Conditions is an Audio-Literature *Possible?*

]o[

CHRISTOPHE FIAT

1. What seems significant to me in Deleuze and Guattari's notion of "*ritournelle*" (or refrain) is that it allows us to consider literature independently of the book. (By book I mean, on the one hand, the cultural artifact (bound in volumes); and, on the other, its artistic and autobiographical pedigree – title, name of author, year of publication, and sometimes its genre.) How does the notion of *ritournelle* do this? The answer is: through the idea of repetition.

2. The type of repetition that interests me here produces an extra-literary space capable of producing effects that no longer depend on writing, nor on language (here I should elaborate further on written language as constitutive of the "book"), but purely on sound. If these effects caused by repetition survive in sound, it is thanks to the sound-track. Also, it is only by refusing to limit itself to the organization of series within the book that repetition can create this extra-literary space. (However subversive, parasitical or playful they might be, these accumulations and reprints of words and sentences in writing constantly come up against the limits of written language.) Repetition also creates new series across media: from the book to the word and from the word to the book. Literature thus projects into the audiophonic space of the sound-track, which extends beyond writing without diminishing its power.

3. With regard to the technique of "*cut-up*," it is repetition that allows us to go beyond the cut to the "jump." The "cut" no longer suffices. Perhaps it never did. OK, the cut is necessary. OK, language must be treated clinically. OK, meaning must be extracted and collective syntax must be sampled. But, this cutting must not stop at transgression; it has to reveal a flux in language and allow us to go beyond writing and the book into a different realm. This sampling is the second procedure involved in the *cut-up*. With its repetition and use of the technique of *cut-up*, the sound-track does not replace the book, but allows language, working through the book as typographic creation, another mode of inscription in which sound is privileged: the temporal and spatial transfer of the voice into sound waves. The sound-track involves finding the right frequency and the mode of expression appropriate to this frequency. (Sound is an extension of the book only if we remain at the lexical and syntactic level of language). This new literature's framework is no longer the book, but the sound-track: no longer the paper leaves, but the link. *Bande/binda*: that which links, the link. Finally, the book could be seen as a sampler. (It is only the book, and not language, that can be sampled). I say "finally" because this is neither a choice, nor merely a good idea; it is a model with real power: the "*sampling book*" or "*sampler.*" The sampler is an analogy that explains how that type of book might work. The book does not in itself sample. Linking the book to the process of sampling merely allows us to: 1) settle a score with those who would have us believe that the voice, the *little* voice, has a proprietorial grip on literature (I am criticizing the sense of ownership and not the voice *per se*); and 2) conceive of the notion of voice in a different way, from the outside to speak. It's time to abandon the myth of the inner voice of the writer struggling to find expression (Romantic fetishism) and our fascination with a voice that enjoys mastery over what it says (dictatorship). The voice I believe in comes from without, not from within. Hence, such a book, surpassed by sound, would function via sampling, not so much on an epistemological level (how could it be since sampling is our model for the book?), but rather on an ethical one: in other words, the book as empty box. This is not a physical emptiness, not an absence of language, but the emptiness that begets emptiness. Such a book would allow an investigation of the affective value of sentences; which lies in their graphic quality.

4. At the outset, the sampler is an empty box whose internal structure is shaped by the desires of the artist or musician. Thus, various sonorities are harmonized within the sampler. In the case of the book, for sonorities read various sentences and words. In the sampler, it is on the material level of sound or language that attractions take place, that everything becomes hybrid and produces an extraordinary type of work: a ULO (Unidentified Literary Object). In the sampling book, the transformation of the sentence into the graphic realm is equivalent to the transfer of sound into waves. What sampling allows is what Wittgenstein failed to understand in "Lecture on Ethics": it is not that an ethics of the book is impossible because such ethics are supernatural and beyond the factuality of existence that ethics requires. It is rather that the type of ethics involved is one of coincidences and encounters, of interactions, of elective affinities which are beyond any type of "natural" determination, a constant questioning of the book as sole keeper of the truth. The book should no longer be allowed a monopoly of the truth, not because of the truth, but because of the monopoly the truth exercises over the book. The fact that the extension of literature into sound is only possible retrospectively (before the sample, one must have the book) does not mean that book and sound are mutually-dependent; on the contrary, what is created is a monstrous time-space lag-gap, an interim in which an ethics of power has the time to produce radical postures like effort, perspicacity, stubbornness, anger, or joy.

5. In the case of the sound-track, the concept of *Hörspiele* appears to me to best sum up such an ethical system. The *Hörspiele* is the form literature takes when it is recorded. In the *Hörspiele*, quotes, expressive vociferations, and background noise are blended in an acoustic space accessible to all because what one hears is a product of interaction, of conversation, and discussion. This is no longer the voice of hopes, dreams, the repressed voice that seems to lurk behind writing, but rather the nakedly physical voice of a larynx in full exertion: a voice with a tone. I am thinking here of Artaud and his radio piece, *Pour en finir avec le jugement de dieu,* but also of the radio programs made by Ezra Pound in fascist Italy. In both cases, what interests me is the misunderstanding linked to the radio broadcast form. In Artaud's case, it is

an ethical misunderstanding: censorship – Artaud's mad excess; in Pound's it is political: Italian fascism – Pound's propaganda. In a way, Artaud and Pound herald Bernard Heidsieck's "action poetry." Heidzsieck explains in *Notes convergentes* that, among other things, the aim of this poetry is to communicate to the audience the tension of a text. I think of this as a warning against any conception of *poésie sonore* (sound poetry) that would seek to free itself utterly of the book. Action poetry seeks to escape the confines of the written book, not by denying the book but by giving the back an autonomy it has never enjoyed (because the book until now has been linked to Truth and the Real, to philosophy and religion). Thus, the book would no longer be a limiting factor on thought, whether in terms of Blanchot's concept of *deuil* (mourning), Wittgentein's "failure", or Bataille's *impossibilité*, but rather as a threshold to be crossed (or not) depending on whether the answers a need: the pragmatic book. The book – via its extension into the realm of sound – could at last encourage multiple readings that would no longer be prescriptive, intimidating, or instructive, but simply hospitable. (In my book on *la ritournelle*, I called this an anti-theory or ambient theory). In the end, the move from book to sound is more motivated by ethics and politics than by esthetics; by the ethical category of fun. Fun is not synonymous with insignificance and triviality. Fun is what allows us to see what is at stake here. Fun allows us to take a risk in order to make the game an autonomous notion. The game is indeed a serious topic that precludes gravity, however. If the game is serious, seriousness can never be a game. (In the end, *Hörspiele* means "listening games"). It is not in order to create a new reading of literature that we must escape from the confines of the book, but to listen to literature in order to grasp the affirmation of life that repetition allows.

6. Listening to the text in this sense is not an effort to bring literature closer to music (which would be to take literature out of one framework (the book) only to put it into another (music), but to push literature into a strange space-time realm whose source and matrix is the sample-book; where the *cut-up* is the rhetoric, and where sound is space. The sound-track only has meaning insofar as it provokes an emotional or existential state that differs from the effect of the book, which only affects internal and silent states of being. These latter states have more to do with a confessional or introspective spirit than with a spirit of expansion. The sound-track creates a new stimulus; language as stimulus. Language no longer acts here by dint of my intention as recognized by the reader, but in a different mode: one of energy influencing emotions and affects. Language creates a physical force whose receptacle is hearing and not the eye, which is usually privileged in written language. In this way, hearing comes fully into its own: a "hear-say" combining in a single system all the senses, including that of sight. And this "live" performance is a practice that allows: 1) the combination of elements linked to several types of expression (cinema, music, plastic arts, dance, literature) and 2) breaks down the distinction between interpreter and creator. (By contrast, the *Hörspiele*, because of the permanency of the recorded reading (sound-track), lacks the openness, plasticity, and micro-political aspects of live performance.) But the fundamental problem of the recording brings us all the same to a reality as rich and inventive as performance. Performance involves the presence of a living being speaking once in his/her name and in the first person. For this reason, performance excludes machine technology unlike the sound-track, which needs programming and delay, but also alterity. The *Hörspiele* is thus at the source of community or new forms of association. As William H. Burroughs explains in "The Invisible Generation," there is so much to be done with the tape recorder: "Les possibilités sont illimitées vous désirez provoquer une émeute placez vos machines dans la rue avec des enregistrements d'émeutes bougez rapidement. . . ." Alterity, which takes the shape here of occupation of urban space, gives existential form to the delay that is essential to recording. This delay is inconceivable without an imagined political community whose end is subversion. The presence of the machine, the matter of the delay, and of the creation of an imagined community creates an abstraction that is not present in performance because the recording is no longer merely a witnessing (a mere audio reception), but has become the essence of the sound. This abstraction is due, I believe, to the very nature of recording itself.

7. In order to understand how this recording functions, we can either turn to Deleuze's model of the rhizome, or to Derrida's model of the gramophone. 1) The rhizome model: of interest here is not so much the rhizome's dimensions and movement as represented on a map, but rather the conversation it generates. There would be no rhizome without the pairing "Deleuze-Guattari": "We wrote *Anti-Oedipe* together. As each one of us was himself plural, that makes a lot of people.... Not in order to get to the point where we no longer say '*I*,' but to the point where it no longer matters whether we say it or not." 2) The gramophone model: not so much the analysis of the gramophone as recording of writing in the most expressive voice, but rather the telephonic experiment carried out by Derrida, which is equivalent to the bipolar experiment undertaken by Deleuze-Guattari. Here is what Derrida says about this experiment: "Up until now, I have talked to you about the letters in Ulysses, about typewriters and telegraphs.... Prior to the act or speech, there was the telephone. In the beginning was the telephone...." The abstraction of the *Hörspiele*, in a certain manner analogous to the abstraction of the book, allows us access to texts that are neither corpuses, nor opuses, nor *live* texts in performance, but texts that are open textual processes, texts that are tendered and offered to us. These are paper-free texts, invisible texts: sound texts. They are all sound, MASTER TAPES OF LITERATURE (so to speak) or voice-overs in an impossible brand of cinema and a non-existent film: voice-overs banishing the hypothetical out of this literature (that is *heard* and not *read*), thus allowing it to exist in a purely sonic frame. Imagine a Godard film without images, or a Duras film without images, or a Kubrick film without images; but without the black or white screens used by Guy Debord in *Hurlements en faveur de Sade* either. Pure sound-track. I think this state created by sound, neither of the book nor of the cinema, may be said to bear similarities to dance.

8. Dance is the only way out for this literature. However, this dance state would neither necessarily require movement (as music would seem to), nor an established presence (as in the case of the book). In order to understand the nature of this dance state, we must revisit the notion of repetition in Deleuze and Guattari's work. First of all, repetition becomes refrain (*ritournelle*) only on the condition that it escapes regression into the past (in the form of obsessive memory), or stagnation in the present (what Guattari calls *l'air du temps* and which resembles stupidity, or at least blind ignorance); in short, on the condition that it projects into the future. In order to understand this anticipatory projection, one must grasp the two ideas at work in repetition: firstly the *reprise*; secondly the *response* (*réplique*). The *reprise* means that, by virtue of the primacy of the *already-there* (the book), every first term is in reality already second. This first term is always made possible or sanctioned by the dominant ideology of its era, which tends to constrain language, inflecting it in a way that makes it a potentially useful tool of social control. The *reprise* is of interest because it creates a zone of rupture, prevents any fetishization of language via, on the one hand, pseudo-naturalistic explanations of its origins; and, on the other, totalitarian celebrations of its *telos*. These are the conditions under which it is possible to conceive of a future that is not inevitable, but merely possible. Hense the necessity of the second idea, the *response* (*réplique*). Once the zone of rupture has been opened, the *response* transforms it into a space of subversion: once the second term has been expressed and given privilege over the first, then comes the ripost, the *response*; in other words the struggle and the effort. While the *reprise* posits ideas, the *response* allows for their exploration. Rupture and exploration of the world combine in this process of repetition, permitting a new understanding of language and things. I thus consider it not at all far-fetched to suggest that dance appears to be the only event that emanates from repetition, by which I mean to the singular elements and specific postures of the dancer, whose sole function is to play with time and space. This is a dance without movement, a dance without presence, a dance that creates a moment of exchange, a situation that allows the speaker who speaks in the voice we hear to claim speech in his own name. Choreography: *la khôra*, or space, in which what is expressed (*graphos*) can be evaluated, conjugated, shared, because it is heard; something that involves understanding in both senses of the word; an event, a singular expression, the product of precise circumstances. Something happens, emerges: the proper noun designating the one who "speaks" and thus makes hearing possible solely by dint of his voice. Due attention must be paid to what he says and how his speech relates to written language. The one who speaks is not an actor, a performer, but, in a sense, a dancer.

9. The *reprise* and the *response*, far from being antagonists, are merely an odd couple that allows a whole new conception of literature to emerge. They allow us to grasp what is singular and irreducible in a work; or, in other terms, a work's creative power that gives life to its monstrous body. While what is known as written language refers to internal structures, what is known as spoken language always speaks about *some thing*. Dance allows the necessary space to imagine an *audio-literature* both catastrophic and epic; no longer a literature anxious about its destiny as language, nor a literature racked by the notion that its thoughts are somehow alienated through being transcribed in the book, but a literature that has found, in the shape of the book and the disk, a final but renewable mode of existence, whose quiet (yet cruel) deliverance would be the epic. In the epic, literature would no longer be the best of all possible discourses, nor a fake concept (an after-thought on the subject of the imaginary), but a morphing backdrop in front of which life could take place: a literature of adventure. While attempting to propose a definition of the epic in his *Theory of the Novel*, Lukacs asks himself: "How can life become essential." In the end, all *audio-literature* tries to answer this question.

○ *Translated by Colin Keaveney*

Panels & Papers

INFLUENCE & PERCEPTION

MATERIAL & CULTURAL SAMPLINGS

POLITICS, FORM & EXPERIMENT

TRANSLATING & (RE)SOURCE

Avant-Garde Poetry & Politics: An "Argument of Insidious Intent"

PAUL VANGELISTI

From the beginning, with German Romanticism and Frederich Schiller, who was reputedly the first to use the term "avant-garde," the notion takes on a political, almost military bearing. At a time when knowledge of the physical world was growing progressively more unstable and fragmentary – beauty itself perhaps a melancholy ruin – Schiller, Goethe, the brothers Schlegel, Novalis and their circle saw poetry as a vital step toward creating the new or avant-garde order. The romantic notion of change and what constituted the "new," with all its attendant forms of primitivism, apocalypse and exoticism, revolved around an essentially poetic individualism. In calling for the destruction of the old order and its defined, social space for poetry, the Romantic writer, a "retrospective prophet" in Friedrich Schegel's words, became a boundless, almost Promethean imagination, outside history, outside prevailing social norms, in short, a political movement or party of one.

In English romanticism, Shelley follows in this political tradition calling the poet "the unacknowledged legislator" of the race. Some 100 years later, Ezra Pound softens the political edge of the rhetoric, adding a scientific cast to the metaphor, when he calls the poet the "antennae of the race." In the Anglo-American tradition, this romanticism of social positioning, the isolate, iconoclastic figure of the avant-garde poet, has, for better or worse, remained with us down through Pound, Charles Olson, Black Mountain, the Beats, the New York School and their descendants of the 1970s and '80s. (Sadly enough, in fact, it was Pound's unlikely defense against charges of treason that he acted completely alone, as an American patriotic movement of one, in making his wartime broadcasts.)

The historical European and Latin American avant-gardes, from 1909–1939, including Futurism, Dadaism and Surrealism, direct their attacks towards the institutions of art and the poet's privileged position, seeking to politicize the maker of verse and return him or her to a more essential place within a dynamic social order. Somewhere on the ideological spectrum from Communism to Fascism, it is important to note that, unlike their Anglo-American counterparts, these poets attempted to integrate their social and aesthetic positions, however zany or naïve some of the initiatives might have been. Their manifestoes took aim at all features of contemporary life, not only literature or the arts.

No less, if not often more extreme in their aesthetic postures, the Anglo-American avant-gardes chose essentially apolitical attitudes. Or, as Renato Poggioli writes in his classic study, *The Theory of the Avant-Garde* (1962), "Especially in certain literary tendencies, Anglo-American extremism is among the most typical and significant expressions of the contemporary avant-garde spirit. But Anglo-American avant-gardism compensates for this by being less theoretical and self-conscious, more instinctive and empirical: the writer in England or America tends, in fact, not so much logically to separate, as obscurely to confound, the problem of the avant-garde and the problem of all modern art."

As we have seen in other panel discussions, the European and Latin American neo-avant-gardes, from the sixties through the eighties, tended to make a connection between what is innovative and/or experimental and what may be considered politically progressive or at least rebellious. Thus, a certain "historical compromise" was reached. Here I am referring, in all sense of the phrase, to a notion first officially enunciated by Italian Communist Party Secretary Enrico Berlinguer, who, in 1973, following the CIA-backed overthrow of the Allende government in Chile, stated that profound historical change could occur without armed revolution. There was in Western Europe another more covert aspect of this compromise, less historical, perhaps, though more practical and laden with sentiment – the sophisticated, if unequivocal support of left-wing social ideology.

Throughout the seventies and eighties, for example, in France, Italy and Spain, summer festivals featured sound, visual and performance poetry, alongside what was then called "linear poetry," under the aegis of the Communist or Socialist administration then in power in a particular provincial city, town or regional government. Sometimes to the embarrassment of these left-wing officials, the neo-avant-gardes took their non-traditional forms of poetry into the streets, town squares, city halls and even, on occasion, insane asylums.

On the question of the political in the avant-garde tradition, all three writers on our panel seem to be more than anything in accord, focusing on poetry's relationship to the public space of language. Each writer has his or her own scenario for an essentially similar goal: from Jean-Michel Espitallier's assumption of the poetic utterance being a subversive "counter-language ... always out of place," to Jennifer Moxley's description of the avant-garde's poetic as adhering to a "politics of *active critique*" (her italics), even Vincent Broqua's reservations about "speaking up," that is, how easily "massified" or integrated within institutional discourse subversive language may become. To enter the *polis*, individualism is not enough. The poet must draw on the art's broadest and perhaps most radical claims: to engage, in Broqua's words, "in redefining poetical language, shattering its boundaries or reinstating old ones with new purposes."

In his "Politics of Poetics," Jean-Michel Espitallier underlines that writing poetry is writing "*in spite of everything*" (his italics). Poetry has become, in social terms, "out of place, that is, obscene (literally *ill-omened*)," inauspicious or repulsive – best kept offstage (*ab scenae*) in the classical, dramatic sense. But he also emphasizes that it is not enough for the poet "to be a foreigner in one's own language." The poet too must be aware of the public or institutional space he is entering, or perhaps better, infiltrating with a strategic and symbolic mission at stake. Strategically, the first move is to make visible "an unacceptable language in a hostile terrain," thus solidifying the language's subversive effect. The second is taking the symbolic next step of scrambling and hijacking the infected codes. As Espitallier characterizes his subversion, using burlesque, grotesque and generally comic effects, he finds "the means to introduce viruses not only into the dominant language, but into the very spirit of the serious," the dominant discourse.

Jennifer Moxley, in her "Notes on Politics, Form & Experiment," assumes a more descriptive approach, trying to isolate what is key in reading very different and diverging avant-gardes, the "ideas and "feelings," as she calls them, associated with avant-gardism. Citing a combination of profound dissatisfaction with the status quo, as well as a certain aggressive mode of addressing the audience, when both attitudes are, according to Moxley, "mixed with an *active critique* of the state (of poetry, of politics, or both)," the result gives rise to that certain " 'avant-garde' feeling."

Beginning with Jacques Roubaud's cautionary and equaling challenging "poetry says nothing," Vincent Broqua is quite careful, in his "Form, Poetry, Politics, a Few Remarks," to define language's public space in as non-sectarian a mode as possible, underlining the difficulty of reaching a contemporary audience with a political or subversive message. Even the most forceful of deliveries, as he notes, may readily become inane in the face of the dominant discourse and its institutionalized public places. Or if confined to literary circles, the questioning voice seems always bound to be addressing the same audience. At one point Broqua finds relief in returning to Roubaud's dictum, with the crucial variation: "poetry just says."

As to form having a political dimension, here one may indulge, I think, in the unfortunate and all too exquisite spectacle of neo-avant-garde writers claiming political urgency for their work simply because they have positioned themselves as experimental or innovative. Curiously enough, both poets and critics in the U.S. who are otherwise institutionalized, that is, living academic, institutional lives, seem most ready to make subversive or radical claims for their writing. The examples are too numerous and embarrassing to cite, except to note that such claims are upheld by an assumption that there is something innately political in the form itself. In all this, one can't help but be aware of drawing dangerously close to a contemporary incarnation of scholasticism that tries to distinguish the essential from the accidental qualities of a form. The potential for qualification and disqualification seem endless, much in the way they were in the sixties in the U.S. with the ultimately fruitless debate between "open" vs. "closed" forms.

All three panelists record some very strong warnings in the area of the politics of form, underscoring the kind of hip orthodoxy or "smart art" that may often result. Moxley puts it most succinctly: "Though many enthusiasts of the avant-garde are invested in being able to draw a straight line from poetry to practical politics, the connection is not evidently compelling."

Espitallier is no less equivocal and somewhat more scathing in his assessment, pointing out, as a serious student of Pierre Bourdieu, how unstable remains the cultural capital created by the neo-avant-gardes: "subversion should not become the rule; the rules of transgression itself must always be transgressed.... You've always got to run faster than the fire." Moreover he notes that the extreme formal complexity and hybrid nature of contemporary poetry refutes categorization and has become in itself, what he calls, "an eminently libertarian space." As once neo-avant-garde notions such as tranversality, hybridization and intergenre mixing approach the status of aesthetic mannerism, they are being emptied of meaning and subversive import: "Taking them for an aim or objective, the powers that be are currently transforming these processes into a sort of neo-academicism that may well produce only sympathetic counterfeits, mere aesthetic reflections of the fantasy of a happy, centrist, non-partisan, and free-trade democracy." The result, for Espitallier, an "avant-garde" in label only, is all the more reassuring for those who control a society's cultural institutions, "in that its strength for breaking and entering will have been sapped by the seduction of an apparently experimental, politically consensual object which is neither too radical nor too conformist. A cool object. A middle of the road aesthetic. Understandably, the institutions are snapping it up."

Vincent Broqua arrives at similar conclusions by examining the use of a conventional form such as the sonnet, and how such "avant-garde *diktat*," as, 'Nowadays, its' impossible to write a sonnet," are based on the false and misleading claim that a particular form is dead and impossible to rediscover. He plays a little game with us, arranging four brief quotations in different fonts and sizes, and asks us if these poems don't appear to be "nowadays." He then reveals that these are from four different poets' recent use of the sonnet, poets (two French and two from the U.S.) "that one likes to consider avant-gardists or poets that have made a very significant contribution to the most radical poetry written in the late twentieth century." Broqua goes on to point out that the problem with the person issuing the anathema against the sonnet arises from a simplistic notion of freedom. As with Espitallier's warnings against "cool art," Broqua underscores the danger that such a notion of freedom may pose precisely in the political arena. As the U.S. was, in April 2003, just beginning its imperial war in Iraq – one recalls the considerable uneasiness hanging over the conference in this regard – Broqua's cautions are indeed remarkable: "What one does with one's freedom and with this word seems to me more important than just to say 'I am free,' 'my verse is free.' As one may see even in this very month of April of 2003, the word freedom is being used and manipulated until it is rid of its basic meaning." Broqua concludes his observations on form by stating that form does not, in and of itself, suppress freedom, nor is one form more inherently conservative than another. Once again echoing Roubaud, he adds: "A form is not, never is, conservative *per se*, it says nothing, it just says."

Finally, as to "experimental poetry" and its relation to the avant-gardes, we have as unstable a proposition as that which treats artistic freedom in formal terms. Is the notion of "experimental" primarily a question of form or does it challenge the nature of poetry itself as it relates to writing? Here it might be useful to look again at Roland Barthes fascinating analysis, in *Writing Degree Zero* (1953), "Is There Poetic Writing?" where he claims that modern poetry after the mid-19th century has become asocial or, as he puts it, "inhuman" writing, cutting the poet off from common literary discourse. Or, recall Walter Benjamin's reflections on modern poetry's rupture with public language, in "The Paris of the Second Empire in Baudelaire." Benjamin remarks that the *l'art pour l'art* of mid-nineteenth century Parisian poetry "gives taste for the first time a dominant position in poetry. In *l'art pour l'art* the poet for the first time faces language the way a buyer faces a commodity on the open market. He has lost his familiarity with the process of its production to a particularly high degree."

Again, all three writers seem to agree as to the essential uselessness of the term "experimental" in respect to innovative poetic practices. For Moxley, the connotations of the term not only have far less historical resonance than the term "avant-garde," but as much as "experimental" might imply "a playful, exploratory spirit," it also carries with it "a wishy-washy uncertainty." Moxley concludes that the notion is not only unhelpful in describing avant-garde practice but also may obfuscate the poet's radical or at least rebellious purpose: "Thus poems created under the rubric of the 'experimental' seem to me, more likely than not, to reduce the purposefulness, that is to say, the *active critique* of the avant-garde gesture, which is not just a series of disruptive formal devices, but a critical stance toward the state and a *very particular* and active content."

Espitallier also comments on the misleading quality of the term, as it may be used "to defuse the innovative force of works that haven't yet invented their reader grid." Or perhaps, more generally stated: "In reality, the experimental seems to me a false debate that incorrectly focuses on what the term covers, just as you can't keep associating avant-garde and totalitarianism or opposing humanism and formalism. As it is used today, this unfortunate word is rather a way of saying what poetry *should be*: risky dealings in the unknown."

Broqua ends his paper with "fourteen clichés, semi-statements, questions and quasi-answers," leaving us to draw our own conclusions. These very astute summations and or, perhaps better, signposts in a treacherous terrain seem not only to encapsulate the critical drift of our panel but also many of the lingering issues that enlivened the conference as a whole:

12 The freedom of form can never be equaled with the freedom of speech. Is one free to speak? What does one do with one's freedom?

14 Mastering constraint amounts to being able to read, being able to decipher the intricacies of a form of a discourse, being able to read isn't that a highly political subject, nowadays? Yet, who reads, who listens right now?

Form, Poetry, Politics – A Few Remarks

VINCENT BROQUA

For Jacques Roubaud poetry "says nothing." If it says nothing how can it be political (politics is about speaking up and acting). Don deLillo in a recent interview says that "writers write because they have to. There doesn't have to be a point." If there isn't a point, what's the point of writing? What's the point then of even considering this notion of form/poetry/writing/avant-garde?

Well, poetry *is* political provided that the word be given its broader and, to me, most relevant meaning: the inscription of one's acts and words in the *polis*. If poetry engages in politics, it does not pass laws or sit at the *conseil des ministres*. To put it blandly, the political space of poetry is not the *Palais Bourbon* or the Congress, but rather the *polis*, society and public space.

Poetry written today is extremely diverse. It can draw on the media and also on the words, the images and the actions of the media. It uses old media/medium/material and sometimes engages in questioning the now with the then. In all situations though, it needs and uses words, signs, sounds, noise, gesture or even posture, in a word, language. Therefore, to label the poetry of the present isn't always easy, "today" is not enough for it does not fully define the poetry I find most challenging. "Contemporary" is equally unsatisfactory a word. How about "avant-garde," or "post-something"? As the discussion after this panel has shown,* the word avant-garde may be repeated over and over again and not say a thing about experimental poetry. Also, the consequence that one may draw from Harold Rosenberg, his *Tradition of the New*, and *The Avant-garde Tradition in Literature* by

* This paper was revised and augmented after the conference.

Richard Kostelanetz, is that both avant-garde and new are no longer accurate to describe the poetry written nowadays. "Experimental," then? Isn't the poetry we like experimental anyway?

The impossibility to fit experimental poetry into a handy, pre-digested term may say something of what this poetry does: it goes against definition (saying this automatically invalidates my own statement). This may be precisely because it engages in redefining poetical language, shattering its boundaries or reinstating old ones with new purposes.

Now, one begins to come back to Roubaud and say: really, poetry says nothing? Well, Roubaud's own answer to this is: "poetry just says."

Through my experience as a Double Change editor and curator of the reading series, I'll try to throw three interlinked remarks into the pan. I am not attempting to solve any question regarding politics, poetic form and experimentation. Perhaps to leave questions open is more unsettling than giving solutions.

1. *Speaking up: voicing one's poetical form in / into the public domain*

In a poetry reading, the poet inscribes his/her voice in the public space. One thinks of (in a consciously ill-assorted way) Bernard Heidsieck, Anne Waldman, McGregor Card, Andrew Maxwell, Jean-Michel Espitallier, Alice Notley, Steve McCaffrey among others. The poet inscribes his/her body and becomes an actor of his text with his voice. More often than not with the poets I just quoted, the form of the poetry reading is part of the poetic form, it extends the poetic form or may even constitute the poetic form. The voice, the tones, the accidental sounds played over or under the reader's voice are the means the poet uses to shape his text. The poet becomes a performer.

Where does this go? One should really question. Did Anne Waldman's defiling of the "rogue state" in the gilded salons of the French Embassy really achieve its aim?* I don't know. What I am sure of though is that reaching

* I'm here referring to a reading Anne Waldman gave at the Cultural Services of the French Embassy in New York on the first night of the Franco-American Poetry Magazine Festival in New York in October 2002.

an audience *is* difficult. It implies more than voicing a text, subversive as it may be. Indeed, the political message is the primary goal of the text, the corrosiveness or the subversive aim of the forceful delivery becomes inane or inapt the moment it is massified, integrated in dominant discourse or in dominant, institutionalized public places. And vice-versa, if a radical voice, a mocking voice, a satirical voice, or a questioning voice remains in the, after all, very small milieu of literary circles, isn't this voice bound to reach always the same audience?

Yet again, I don't know. Other forms of art give us a clue as to how form may be at the same time inscribed in public space and question by its very inscription: visual artists such as Raymond Hains, Gonzalez-Torres, Claude Rutault for instance inscribe their work in public space and try via this form to question the place of art in the public domain. The gesture itself is part and parcel of the form if the piece of art and sometimes even defines it.

2. *Disobedience*

My whole argument revolves around disobedience or how to escape dominant discourse or dominant ideas via poetry. The question of form is germane to that of politics. *Disobedience* is the title of Alice Notley's 2002 collection (I take Notley here because her collection is a good example of a path in poetry that one can also detect in Nicole Brossard, Rachel Levitsky, Jennifer Moxley or Harryette Mullen, different as they are). As always, political discourse is a forte in Alice Notley's collection, yet what interests me is that she should have chosen as a form of disobedience the overlapping of two forms – novel fiction and diary/poetry – combined to a strong feminine radical voice. When one reads statements like "All detectives take drugs – Chirac, write your own / prescription and fill it," of course one feels like saying Alice Notley is political. But it is not this immediate political quality that seems to me most remarkable in Alice Notley's work. In fact, her work is political in the broader sense of the word (again) through the ever changing name of one of the *personae* Hardwood and the constant degrading slips on his name, "Dante and Hardon I mean Hardwood," "Hardwill," "Hugh I mean huge Hardwood." Language is constantly questioning itself and the defining moment that seems to be coextensive of the use of language. Of course, one may object as was done at the end of the panel* that the gender barriers etc are also questioned in Hollywood movies and series, but are we really talking of the same thing here? I am still to find a movie that does what the multifaceted form of Alice's poem does: Hollywood movies (but I may be too French here) do not question these barriers, they seem to do so in a way that may gently unsettle the viewer. Nothing like the restless identity of the "I" in Notley's poem. The "I" becomes a cipher "E" which is also the name of Alice E. Notley, which is also the final /i:/ of Dante, which is also "E for seal. For Spell. For suppression," which is "him":

> E has arms, gesticulates apparently speaking
> no one can hear him.
>
> E is what questions language:
>
> Language uninhabited,
> just a quick
> fix. a surface. reject him.

I think it is not altogether unreasonable to say that what Alice Notley's poetic form allows can never be achieved in Hollywood movies.† This questioning of the boundaries between genres (novel, story, poem, diary),

* In the discussion after the panel, one person objected that questioning gender barriers was not as such a feature of experimental poetry. This person argued that gender barriers are also deconstructed in Hollywood movies, which I am willing to grant on a very surface level, but, as I all too briefly state above, Hollywood movies (or at least the ones I have in mind) do not compare in any way with what Alice Notley's text does.

† She refers to Demi Moore in one of the poems of the collection but as she said in an essay: "Sometimes it seems that the worst consequence of the modern split between poetry and story has been the emergence of pure action, pure violence, as the major mass genre, as in movies, novels, TV."

between biography, autobiography, fiction, between "he" and "she" creating a "heshe" seem to me to construct the disobedience the title refers to. Form is the object of disobedience not so much because Notley rejects form, but because she engages fully in it and plays with various instances of forms.

3. Forme contrainte *and freedom of form*

Questioning form, debunking form from the inside or playing with form is what Notley does. Is that political? I would like to return to my general argument by narrowing down my last remark to a traditional poetic form: the sonnet. Yes, the sonnet, this archaic, conventional, conservative form. Why on earth should I want in a paper like this to talk about the sonnet? What avant-garde, politics and poetic form have to do with the sonnet?

My will to talk about the sonnet is partly prompted by a *diktat:* a person made a comment to me that ran approximately thus: "Nowadays, it's impossible to write sonnets." Before saying anything, let's devise and play a little game. Read these four poems in these four different fonts*:

First poem:

> Corolla corona, bliss-bane – delay
> surge and sediment. Say instrument and gash
> and ruminant remnant. Rex the ruse. Be dead.

Second poem:

> Morbid tint of glass the hooker's glance
> The crossed-out phrases the mechanical ass
> Oasis of Arabs hawking t-shirts and maps.

* My fonts.

Third poem:

> *Onze novembre, achèvement sous la pluie de*
> *l'antéfixe des oiseaux.*
> *Dans cette phrase, ce sont les espaces entre les*
> *mots qui m'ont donné l'ordre des mots*

Forth poem:

> **Debout, en habit noir**
> **Canne dans sa main gauche, haut de forme à droite**
>
> **Perruque blanche, souliers pointus turlutu**
> **Tu.**

What do you see here? Can you try to date these poems or say roughly whether you would apply the word "nowadays" to them?

I suppose that you would at least label one of these poems with "nowadays." And you probably understood by now that these lines are all excerpts from sonnets; and sonnets written not so long ago respectively by Karen Volkman (2001), Paul Vangelisti (1983), Emmanuel Hocquard (1998) and Jacques Roubaud (2003).

"Nowadays, it's impossible to write sonnets": what is at stake in this statement is the false claim that a form is dead or that it is impossible to use what's been used before. In the mind of the person that issued this anathema is, I suppose, a false notion of what freedom may be. What one does with one's freedom and with this word seems to me more important than just to say "I am free," "my verse is free." As one may see even in this very month of April of 2003, the word freedom is being used and manipulated until it is rid of its basic meaning.

Form does not suppress freedom, form isn't conservative because of the wrong assumption that to write in a determined genre or form means to write as one did a hundred, two or three hundred years ago. If one thing, the four poems quoted above clearly show that one can question the form from the inside, and I find it fascinating that poets that one likes to consider avant-gardists or poets that have made a very significant contribution to the most radical poetry written in the late twentieth century should engage with a form like this. That they should try to define and use their freedom with words, language, sounds, images, page, concreteness from the inside of the *forme contrainte* also establishes the sonnet as an experimental form of the twentieth, and twenty-first century. De facto, these poets give the lie to the widespread idea that a constraint of form amounts to a fixed form, i.e. a form cast once and for all in an everlasting mould of marble or concrete. A form is not, never is, conservative *per se*, it says nothing, it just says.

I will end this paper with these fourteen clichés, semi-statements, questions and quasi-answers and you will make the links. Let me make this clear, this is no ABC of form, *this* is not a poem:

1 "Nowadays" is new, *cela va plus avant*, or is it already old and withered as I utter the word?
2 Avant-garde is the opposite of arrière-garde, why war? PS: Dada, is this a horse I'd like to ride or has it been ridden too many times nowadays?
3 Berrigan, Roubaud, Mayer, Volkman, Hocquard, Vangelisti, Moxley all lost to the cause? (They all experiment with sonnets, among other things, even nowadays).
4 14 vers, 14 lignes, why should I decide that this fits into 14 lines? Why not? NB: "Avant-garde. Elitist. Mention military origin of the term as though that says it all. Use interchangeably with experiment, innovative, alternative and then add "tradition."*

5 Impossible. Impassible. Imprévisible. *Impertinent. Impish*: où nous entraîne la contrainte?
6 "Form straight-jackets me into not being able to write, suppresses my freedom" (a student to Michael Palmer).

* *The Dictionary of Received Ideas*, 1997, eds. Bouvard and Pécuchet.

7 Breaking with convention from inside the form: reformation or revolution? PS: can you organise dissent from the inside of a structure: that's called *noyautage* from *noyau*, "kernel." What's the kernel of a sonnet?

8 Can poetry change one's life?, can a sonnet change one's life?: that's too much like a question for an essay, I don't like these questions, essay is a form of constraint, though.

9 Form frees me (*où l'on entend* freeze).

10 "But make no mistake," Bush Senior, "this aggression will not stand" "We will free the Iraqi people, this danger shall be removed," Bush Jr. who reads? Who remembers?

11 "Why can't people use pooper-scoopers," "Could one remove the danger that these tramps constitute: why not place them in a mental-home where they would be safe and sound and warm and fed and I could wear my pearl necklace out in the street," actually heard in the 14th Parisian *arrondissement*, first pseudo-democratic "conseil de quartier" between the two runs of the 2002 French Presidential election.

12 The freedom of form can never be equaled with the freedom of speech. Is one free to speak? What does one do with one's freedom?

13 "If the poet is conventional about form, form is doomed to be conventional" (Michael Palmer to the student).

14 Mastering constraint amounts to being able to read, being able to decipher the intricacies of a form of discourse, being able to read isn't that a highly political subject, nowadays? Yet, who reads, who listens right now?

Politics of Poetics

JEAN-MICHEL ESPITALLIER

Every literary object connects an individual experience to a collective grammar, a vision of the world to the world; it reverts to it, adds to it, aggravates it, because literature is genetically programmed to set its deviant grammars against the dominant language. Style is basically a form of conflict. The work sets up a frictional zone between myself and the world, a zone replete with short circuits, play, and states of war, which are always political zones initially. Under this assumption, poetry takes on a special status. Its dangerous qualities rest first on the weakness of its audience. In other words, due to its virtually non-existant spectacular/mercantile weight, poetry has become a point of breaking and entering, which is only an extension into the City of the breaking and entering it commits in language. Its very status excludes it from market laws, media injunctions, the fetishism of transparency and fantasies of connection. Ultimately, we might suppose that in escaping from the tyranny of the utilitarian (and this includes the question we are asking here today), the gratuity of art for art's sake represents a fundamentally subversive act, even if that would force us to consider the principle of intention (which distinguishes the revolutionary from the rebel), which brings us back to the question of commitment.

So, to write poetry is to write *in spite of everything*. It is also to infect language with a counter-language that resists canon law, since the latter puts the object/poem in a situation of tension and crisis that must be resolved at the very moment of provocation, situations that Deleuze has dubbed "bottlenecks." Poetry is always out of place, that is, obscene (literally *ill-omened*); it *damages* a context which, by its very nature, is hostile to it. Attacking language amounts to destroying a heritage that guarantees the values and customs that hold our modern societies together: gregarity, sedentarity, sociocultural levelling, liberal model, etc. Thus, linguistic dysfunctions (the Baudelairian uncanny, for example), reach well beyond the sphere of language and the question of the beautiful. They mark out autonomous and non-aligned zones or points of "resistance to the amphitheater" as Sloterdijk put it, and create other value systems, or more precisely the possibility of other value systems, for those who wish to see them. This is called utopian reason.

Yet the confinement in which poetry finds itself actually reduces its strike range and speed of metastasic proliferation. Hence the need to extract it from its cocoon, to infiltrate associated, foreign spaces, to smuggle it in, to scramble codes and jump borders, to displace both gaze and sites, etc. It is not enough to be a foreigner in one's own language, to form a wrinkle, tumor, or scrape, though it is appropriate to import this strangeness into the context to be contaminated, which after all is the first condition of any infectious process. The stakes are two: first strategic – it allows us to reveal an unacceptable language in a hostile terrain, and this visibility condenses the subversive effect; then symbolic – it scrambles and hijacks infected codes. These positions do indeed have their aesthetic and formal translations: the hijacking, the cut-up, the ready-made, and the sample, among other techniques, unglue, withhold, commandeer, and/or kidnap elements in order to exile, graft, or clone them, thus proposing different ways of cropping and redistributing the real, and giving critical rereadings of it. For my part, in the resources of the burlesque, the grotesque extravagance, and the comic, whose diabolically subversive force was demonstrated by Baudelaire, I find the means to introduce viruses not only into the dominant language, but also into the very spirit of the serious, into the very Jesuitical quibbling of academic or avant-garde hortodoxy which, forcing the self-surveillance and conformity of a compulsory and alienated anticonformism on us, always presents itself as a fascistic language. The enemy is obviously never in the place of representation as we imagine it to be.

These writing processes are thus doubly political: first by revealing the dominant language and its shortcomings, enticements, conceits, empty syllogisms, and alienating mechanisms; then as a means of conquering autonomous spaces of resistance, this conquest being inseparable "from all forms of aesthetic rupture," as Pierre Bourdieu made clear. Another essential point: subversion should not become the rule; the rules of transgression itself must always be transgressed. A work can only be truly subversive at this price and its anticonformity must be constantly challenged, outstripped by the swift digestion of societies. You've always got to run faster than the fire.

Another thing. The decline and blurring of codes that up to the age of Romanticism allowed us to "recognize" poetic form have lead to such a high degree of formal complexity, to such phenomenonal hybridity and deterritorialization that this form, in that it refutes categorization, has become an eminently libertarian space. The transversality, the hybridization, the intergenre mix – which are natural forms for many of us (I personally claim them as necessary means to an end) – are its most apparent formal symptoms, but these notions are gradually being emptied of meaning through overuse and abuse. Taking them for an aim or objective, the powers that be are currently transforming these processes into a sort of neo-academicism that may well produce only sympathetic counterfeits, mere aesthetic reflections of the fantasy of a happy, centrist, non-partisan, and free-trade democracy. One third prose, one third verse, one third cut up and a fourth or even a fifth third of whatever else you might want (image, sound, salt dough), a door open on a middle course which is all the more reassuring in that its strength for breaking and entering will have been sapped by the seduction of an apparently experimental, politically consensual object which is neither too radical nor too conformist. A cool object. A middle of the road aesthetic. Understandably, the institution is snapping it up.

A word on the experimental issue. This highly elastic notion is problematic because any writing that thinks, however little, about its form (and the experimental is always initially understood in formal terms) belongs to this false category. Thus the experimental might be to the poet what prose is to M. Jourdain. Each adaptation of new writerly procedures is a cell of experimentation, "thousands of little inventions without histories" that art historian André Chastel spoke of.

The notion of the experimental covers a variety of practices all of which seek new tools to make the language resonate differently. So I'm speaking more of designations ("experimental" might have replaced "avant garde") and even of labels, which are occasionally used pejoratively to defuse the innovative force of works that haven't yet invented their reader grid. A hypothesis: every experimental form is (or makes) poetry (in the broadest meaning of the term), but all poetry is not experimental (and this leads us again to ponder the definition of this highly dilated genre). In reality, the experimental seems to me a false debate that incorrectly focuses on what the term covers, just as you can't keep associating avant garde and totalitarianism or opposing humanism and formalism. As it is used today, this unfortunate word is rather a way of saying what poetry *should be*: risky dealings in the unknown.

◦ *Translated by Guy Bennett*

Notes on Politics, Form, & Experiment

JENNIFER MOXLEY

Having just published an essay "On Content" in the Canadian magazine *Open Letter*, I couldn't help but be pleasantly amused to be, shortly thereafter, asked to participate in a panel on *form*. These two interdependent categories – form and content – are only separated, I have recently and naively discovered, at one's extreme peril. That said, I would now like to briefly discuss how the *formal* poetics of the avant-garde, that much politicized artistic sub-group, tends to give rise to a very specific kind of *content*, which in turn produces a very specific type of artistic experience.

In addition to its historical positioning, what exactly makes a poem "avant-garde," or conjures up the essence of "avant-gardism"? Before launching into his celebrated definition of the "gothic" Ruskin, with typical respect for the awesomeness of the achievements he was about to whittle down into words, well describes the problem facing any would-be "definer" of an artistic style: "The principal difficulty," he writes, "arises from the fact that every building of the Gothic period differs in some *important* respect from every other." The key word here being "important," insomuch as the *difference* of one gothic structure from another is not a casual thing, this "difference" may make *all* the difference. He then goes on to say that the character of the "gothic" goes beyond vaulted arches and stained glass – for many buildings may have these attributes. What makes a building truly gothic is a careful mingling of several ideas coming together in such a way as to "have life." In other words, to evoke, in its very structure, the "feeling" that one associates with *gothicness*. But how does this relate to the avant-garde poem?

When I shuffle my thoughts back through the various energetic poetic "vortices" that one might group under the heading "avant-garde" – symbolists, futurists, dadaists, language poets, and so on – I cannot help but think that the difference of each from the other, that is, what makes each group unique, is *key*, and yet at the same time I'm mindful of the fact the reading poems produced by these vortices often causes similar "ideas" and "feelings" – "ideas" and "feelings" that I associate with avant-gardism – to arise in my mind. Such that I may turn to Rimbaud's "Qu'est-ce pour nous, mon cœur" and read

> Tout a la guerre, à la vengeance, à la terreur,
> Mon esprit! Tournons dans la morsure: Ah! passez,
> Républiques de ce monde! Des empereurs,
> Des régiments, des colons, des peuples, assez!

[All to war, to vengeance and to terror, / My spirit! Let us turn about in the biting jaws. Ah! vanish, / Republics of this world! Of emperors, / Regiments, colonists, peoples – enough!]

for the very same reasons that I turn to Mayakovsky to read

> Don't give me Hegel
> and his dialectic!
> It smashed its heads
> together
> And the sound
> of the skulls cracking
> was poetry!
> Like fame and genius
> going down
> the same drain!
> Ok! Poems go
> down drain
> too!
> Hundreds of trillions of people

down the drain
into heaven!
To hell with statues
and monuments.
We're famous enough."

Or, (to cite a contemporary example) the inverse address produced by the savage irony in Kevin Davies'

Even while the moneyless
Parasites of America are held down while
a bipartisan congress takes shits in their mouths
For immigrants American is full of mysteries
Who to eat
Where to invest....

Now all three poets, Rimbaud, Mayakovsky, and Davies, are formally distinct and yet all evince certain qualities that I associate with the avant-garde. They all seem dissatisfied with "things as they are," not just in *art* but in the larger society, and they all have a very particular mode of *address*, a sort of combination *cri du cœur* and "slap in the face of public taste," like that of a pissed-off adolescent with a Cassandra complex who is alert to hypocrisy and wants to condemn it, while caring as little for his own life as for any punishment you might exact upon him.

Perhaps then, the singular forcefulness of such an address when mixed with an *active critique* of the state (of poetry, of politics, or both) is what gives rise to that "avant-garde" feeling I described above. And perhaps the "active critique" part of this equation has as its goal something rather lofty, almost utopian, that is: the total transformation of art, life, and even consciousness itself as all have been proposed by the powers of the modern era – whether they take the form of the fascist extremist, the capitalist do-gooder, or the seemingly benign bourgeois philistine – all defined as "enemies" of art at one time or another by avant-gardists such as these. Proclaiming the "end" of the avant-garde, as people have been wont to do in my lifetime, while these elements of society still thrive, is tantamount to admitting defeat by the "getters and spenders" (as Wordsworth so astutely defined them), and marching, like zombies in a 1950s horror flick, willingly to receive those "mind-forged manacles" Blake so ominously spoke of.

In the interest of refining my definition a bit, let me also say that, of course, there may be poems or poets who want to change the society who are *not* avant-garde, like those well-meaning socialist poets so popular in the '30s, or Calvin Trillin writing doggerel for *The Nation*. And there may be poets who press their poetry into the *service* of resistance in times of crises, as so many poets began to do post 9/11, who are not avant-garde. And there may be poets who want to "disturb" the definition of art and yet are not avant-garde. Here I might evoke a writer like Mallarmé or even Ashbery. These poets may suffer a reception very similar to that of the avant-garde, being shunned, mocked or accused of "nonsense," while never having set out to achieve those "goals." These poets may create poems that are quite astonishing and wonderful, poems that may even change the lives of their readers, and yet still they are not likely, upon reading, to create that "avant-garde" feeling I described above. And finally, there are those poets who do not set out to change anything, but end up changing everything, for possessed of a radical consciousness their poems represent reality in a wholly new way. Here I might name Blake, Dickinson, Smart, Khlebnikov, or even Rimbaud in his *Illuminations*. Such visionaries are often adopted as "honorary members" by more self-conscious avant-gardes; in fact, their work might even fit the "definition" of avant-garde to a tee. But there is always something more going on in the poetry of such visionaries, a powerful moment of complete and total disregard for the value scales of this world, an insight beyond the normal concerns of everyday existence such that the typical methods of rebellion would seem almost childish in the face of it. It is this "something more" that often makes such writers appear, to the casual observer, otherworldly or insane.

"Experiment" is something different altogether. It's a word with far less historical resonance, a word that is rather vague in its connotations as regards poetry. "Experiments" can simply be things one does not know the outcome of, or they can be related to experience, that which is attempted or tried. These connotations contain both a playful, exploratory spirit to them as well as a wishy-washy uncertainty. Do you really *believe* that or are you just experimenting? Combined with the word poetry, "experimental" seems sometimes to simply mean "difficult to read," other times to mean "self-conscious of its devices," though some poems can be both of these things and still fall short of being "experimental." To me the word falls most easily into understanding when used to describe what Oulipians do, namely generate poetry out of predetermined formal constraints. Thus poems created under the rubric of the "experimental" seem to me, more likely than not, to reduce the purposefulness, that is to say, the *active critique* of the avant-garde gesture, which is not just a series of disruptive formal devices, but a critical stance toward the state and a *very particular* and active content.

Though many enthusiasts of the avant-garde are invested in being able to draw a straight line from poetry to practical politics, the connection is not evidently compelling. For while setting out to measure the distance between one's *intentions* and one's *effects* may be a perfectly reasonable quest in some disciplines, in poetry, so often removed from its ideal audience by scores of years, it can be an especially frustrating endeavor. Which is not to dismiss the importance of discussing poetry as a political art. After all, if we take Aristotle's idea that to be "political" means only that it is needful and beneficial to live in states, then the definition of the "political" becomes greatly expanded and, suddenly, all who strive to keep civil life from losing its original purpose of preserving man's necessary liberty may be properly thought to be "political." Even poets who, on the surface, appear to be quite removed from any practical politics may fall into this camp, allowing aesthetes and naysayers who withdraw into the rarefied space of *l'art pour l'art* to be read *politically*.

My notes have said nothing so far of that special subcategory of politics, experiment, and form: the "politics of poetry." Here I might invoke what seems to me an increasingly popular trend, no doubt fostered by the growing industry of creative writing in the academy. Of late I have noticed that the poet as artist or bohemian is being overtaken by the poet as "professional," that is to say, by writers who, like many novelists, try to create a viable product that will easily insert itself into the already existing definitions of the literary market. No doubt this type of poet has always existed, and in truth I see nothing wrong with trying to earn one's living through one's chosen medium, but if the cash and laurels on offer undermine the poets' desire to represent the present reality in artistic form, no matter the risks and notwithstanding the fashions, then poetry would certainly cease to be political, however narrow or broad our definition of that word, in any meaningful or helpful way.

I've tried here to show that, from the standpoint of a politics of *active critique*, the avant-garde poetic is certainly the most immediately satisfying, and that work falling under this category is not merely concerned with "formal" questions in poetry, but with a particular content, or mode of address. On the other hand, poetry "experiments," while certain to generate satisfying aesthetic objects on occasion, strike me as *less* politically forceful than intentionally made poems. And professionals ... well, their fame is not likely to endure. Perhaps then it is the visionaries, those poets who are able to create new forms through which to see the less transient truths of any immediate moment, that may, in the end, prove the most liberating, and therefore the most political of all.

Panels & Papers

INFLUENCE & PERCEPTION

MATERIAL & CULTURAL SAMPLINGS

POLITICS, FORM & EXPERIMENT

TRANSLATING & (RE)SOURCE

Translating & (Re)Source: Introductory Notes

GUY BENNETT

This conference, the exhibit it celebrates, and the book on which the exhibit is based are all predicated on the practice of translation, and the presence here of the various participants should serve to remind us that poets themselves are often also translators of poetry. Some poets – Octavio Paz, for example – have argued that there is no essential difference between translating a poem and writing one, the implication of that position being that all writing is a form of translation.

As we researched and wrote *Charting the Here of There*, Béatrice and I discovered a number of cases that seem to both demonstrate that hypothesis, and take it one step further. I am thinking of situations in which a poet takes a translation he has done as a point of departure for new writing. There were poems by Ron Padgett, for example, translated into French by Serge Fauchereau. Padgett later retranslated those translations back into English, thus creating a new set of complementary poems, which Fauchereau then used as the basis of his "Variations sur un thème de Ron Padgett," which are translations/rewritings of Padgett's translations of his translations of Padgett. And then there's Michael Palmer's "Baudelaire Series," translated into French by Emmanuel Hocquard. Having finished the translation, Hocquard kept on writing, creating a new work, his *Théorie des tables*, which Michael Palmer later translated into English. (To step outside the domain of French poetry for a moment, we could add that Jerome Rothenberg wrote his *Lorca Suites* in much the same way, writing through his translation of Lorca's *Suites* to compose a new work.)

If I may give an example from personal experience, about twelve years ago I became fascinated – obsessed, actually – with the work of Michelle

Grangaud and began translating it, publishing my translations in American poetry journals. One such translation appeared, along with some of my own poems, in a short-lived magazine called *Faucheuse* (named, coincidentally, for French book designer Pierre Faucheux). When Michelle received a copy of the magazine, she was intrigued by the constraint I had used in my pieces and subsequently translated them into French. She then went on to use that constraint as a point of departure for a new text, which later appeared in the literary supplement of *Le Monde*. I saw this latter piece in the paper, and wrote a new work based on it, by applying a variant of the same constraint to her piece that she had borrowed from mine. The resulting poem doesn't resemble either of our work, oddly enough, though it was written by both of us in an exchange that grew out of mutual translation.

As far as I know, the exchange stopped there, but I've never stopped thinking about it, since this type of back and forth poses some interesting questions about the nature and role of translation and its relationship to writing, and, more specifically, about the relationship between the quote unquote original text and its translation. We have asked our panelists to consider these questions in their talks here today.

One Story / One Rumor / Through the Fact of Translation

BENJAMIN HOLLANDER

Guy and Beatrice have asked:

"What is the original text in translation?"
"What is the nature of collaboration in translation?"
"What, exactly, is the relationship between source and target text changing?"

(so, among all these poets and translators, I'll begin with a simple claim)

I am no translator. I am (the) other, the source of someone else's beautiful or miserable translation.

There's little work in being the source of someone else's translation, something Walter Benjamin instinctively knew when he refused to call his classic essay "The Task of the Translated."

I don't mind being translated – in fact, I look forward to it in precisely the same way one anticipates returning home. In other words, or in the other's words, being translated is a personal story, sometimes an extension of a family story, as if my poetry might not have a home without it.

Guy and Beatrice have asked: What is the original text in translation? But given the story I'm about to tell, I can only ask: What is the original text if not in translation? In other words, for me, how could it exist otherwise but in the other language – first?

This is not an academic story. This is not a "my poetics" story. It's a much more personal story inscribed in my book, *The Book of Who Are Was*, a collection of poems where characters or figures – like letters – traverse time, encounter each other, correspond, and appear and disappear, as words do in translation.

As it was written, the book depended on a hope and a question:

How would a future reader be implicated in the theatre of its writing, as if in collaboration with the writer?

Or more to the point: how would the family history I told within it reach this reader, so that the book itself would become a corresponding family history between me and another who found (herself in) it outside the time of its writing.

This (therefore) will have been the story about the nature of collaboration in translation, the family story of Oscarine and Jacques and me.

Oscarine and Jacques and me

In 1992, I am invited to the Fondation Royaumont to have excerpts of my unpublished manuscript, *The Book of Who Are Was*, translated by a collective of translators. The book begins with a citation from the philosopher Jacques Derrida, which reads in translation: "This (therefore) will not have been a book." Other words of his are embedded in my narrative.

Among the translators at Royaumont in 1992 is Oscarine Bosquet, who takes up the task of finishing the translation of the text once I leave the collaborators at Royaumont.

Oscarine and I correspond over the years, in which time she marries. In 1997, six months before the book is published in English with Douglas Messerli's Sun & Moon Press, a condensed French version appears under Oscarine's signature. It's certainly not the first time a translation exists as a published book while the original is still forthcoming. Still, I wonder: What – and where – is the original text if not in translation? And how could it exist otherwise but in the second language first?

When the book is issued in English, I send a copy to the philosopher Jacques Derrida, whom I don't know but who writes me a beautiful note. I wonder, however: which book is he admiring? He must, I assume, have seen the French edition six months earlier. He must have seen it, I assume, not because he knows who I am as a poet, but because he knows who the translator has become over the years: the translator Oscarine Bosquet who has – yes – married the son of the philosopher Jacques Derrida whose words "This (therefore) will not have been a book" are cited in translation in Benjamin Hollander's *The Book Of Who Are Was*, a book the hope of which depended on how future readers would be implicated in the theatre of its writing as if in collaboration with its writer or, more to the point, on how its writer and its future readers would make of the book itself a corresponding family history found outside the time of its writing, as have Oscarine and Jacques, who have written with me: "This (therefore) will not have been a book," never only a book, never only an academic story, but a much more personal story about the nature of collaboration in translation:

How could the book exist otherwise?

like a rumor
for
Juliette and Emmanuel and me
re: the question
"What, exactly, is the relationship between source and target text changing?"

Did I tell you I was born in Israel? Well, I'll get back to it, as one source. In the meantime, let me say:

If I am the source of someone else's translation, how does the translation change me and the poem?

The source of my poem "Onome" was sounded in the dark: I turned off the lights, the appliances, double locked the door, drew the curtains, and I started writing without seeing the words before me. After a half hour, I switched on the lights. Letters were spiraling and circling into each other on the page. I saw three syllables over and over, which I pronounced Onome, almost like an omen: Onome Onome Onome. It sounded like a figure on the run, like a rumor. A scare tactic in the dark. It worked.

It worked so well that I lost sight of the three words actually spelled out before me – not "Onome," but O No Me, a startling bit of self-recognition, as if the whole time I had sounded "Onome" I couldn't know or see the "me" in it, as if the word scared me out of my own skin. Is this what Oppen meant when he said: "When the man writing is frightened by a word, he may have started." I started it – like a rumor.

When Emmanuel Hocquard and Juliette Valéry saw it, their translation and publication of this poem started another rumor which changed it.

In English, the poem is 2–3 pages. In French, it's almost the same. Yet the rumor I hear suggests its reception among the French, and thus maybe its status, is different, different enough to have changed it in English.

In French, the small poem has appeared as a small book. This is Juliette's chapbook – her Format Americain series. But it was only a small poem, only a few pages when I started it.

In French, I hear, it is sometimes taught, the way a book is sometimes taught.

In French, it has appeared in several anthologies of American poets in translation and one time, most curiously, in an anthology of mostly French poets. In English, my poetry has not appeared in even one anthology of mostly American poets.

In French, it's been critiqued in a review of "detective novels in France," as if it were a book, a novel, long: the reviewer called it "a detective poem," a "*poème policier*," a genre unto its own, I suppose.* Maybe that's why, being a genre of its own in French, no one needs to call it much of anything in English. These are the rumors I hear about its reception in French, in translation, so how does the fact of this translation change my small poem in English? And, if we are charting the here of there, how does its "thereness" in French affect this small poem here in English.

Well, I make it – what else – a book, the book in English it never intended to be – that is, seeing how Emmanuel and Juliette have spread the word of this 2–3 page poem like a rumor through the fact of translation, I write 30 more pages. I follow their lead. And partly because of them, I perpetuate the rumor I started.

* Alain Chareyre-Méjan, "L'écrivain, le cancre, le privé," in *Formes policières du roman contemporain* (Paris: la licorne, 1998), p. 40

"Onome" the name becomes a character. It turns into a figure of speech, "Onoma", the contraction of a Greek phrase meaning "the Being that is avidly sought." On the run. Like a rumor. It lurks under the sign of "anomie," the name for what Emile Durkheim calls urban lawlessness. A figure on the run like a rumor in Durkheim's urban lawlessness, it transforms into the detective poem it never intended to be. In English, it incarnates the atmosphere of the poem the French reviewer said was like experiencing someone "after an evening of drinking, when one is too much seeing things ahead of their representations."* As if it's always discovering the name it could be but is not. As in translation:

where, Emmanuel says (and I cite it) "language itself can turn to rumour." And so it does with Onome, which generates a long companion sequence called "Levinas and the Police" – where another Emmanuel – Levinas – follows like a rumour what the first Emmanuel – Hocquard – started. With me. With Juliette. With Emmanuel, who has written: "To translate American poetry into French is to gain ground," so that "the surface area" of French literature "is expanded into unexplored zones.... Unowned territory. No man's land." "No French poet could ever write this," he says.† Yes, I agree: "No French poet could ever write this." But having been born in Israel and given my particularly accented and ambiguous relation to American English, I have to say about my poetry a fact Emmanuel already knows: that "no American could ever write this."‡ Which, if my poetry is read in translation more hospitably than it is at home, makes for a startling bit of non-self (or nonsense) recognition: that "no French poet could ever write this which no American [poet] could ever write." This No-man's land and this No-One Land: this being in the poetry of the extraterritorial or, to use Giorgio Agamben's phrase, "reciprocal extraterritorialities."

Is this the ideal political poetic imaginary? A curious state to be in which is, curiously, not a state at all but a future condition (*État*),"unowned territory" which is neither French nor American but is negotiated by the

* Ibid., p.41

† Emmanuel Hocquard, "Blank Spots," http://epc.buffalo.edu/orgs/bureau/tb_a.html, p. 3.

‡ Ibid, p. 4

rumor of a poetry which emerges from both, or, if I think about the territory where I am really from – the source of my sources – would neither be called Israel nor Palestine but the rumor of a land emerging from both, a future condtion (*État*) which seeks the name it could be but is not.

As in translation.

Translation/Transmission: Lines of Flight Beyond Pound & Mallarmé

PIERRE JORIS

1. The aim of this brief presentation is to make a pitch for the need to foreground areas of non-metropolitan France – in this case more specifically the Maghreb – as vortexes of imaginative energies in need of translations & as loci of poetic lines of flight more vital & to the point for an American poetics today than the translation, no matter how valuable in itself or how aesthetically pleasing it may be, of yet another neo-Mallarmean Parisian.

2. Sick, dying or dead empires, lose their centripetal pull & the energies remain, are allowed to, or do so under their steam, to remain in or on, or return to, the margins. Come to think of it isn't that exactly where the most vital energies have always been located anyway – empire is in fact nothing more than the sucking vortex that pulls the best inward, to Rome, Beijing, Paris, London, New York. Don't forget that Li Po was born from exiled parents probably in Western Turkistan & grew up in Sichuan; a dialect from the frontier of the empire was most likely his mother tongue, and not the language he would write in later. Or think of Ovid who was born and raised in the city of Sulmo, was thus Paelignian, a non-Latin Italic. And in England, after Pound left & Eliot moved from the bank teller job into the Church of England and Faber & Faber – or did he move the bank into Faber & Faber, or Faber & Faber into the Bank, or both Faber & Faber and the Bank into the Church, whatever, from then on there wasn't any poetry worth speaking of being written in the thing called England, i.e. in London and the home counties (excepting for the cocktail chatter of Auden & Co.) until that short interlude of the sixties & seventies. All the interesting work was being done by & at the edges of empire: by Bunting in Norththumbria or Persia or the Canaries, wherever he happened to be (& published in Texas); by David Jones, the Welshman, by MacDiarmid the Scot. And when Paris lost it, & Breton was on his way to New York, the boat stopped in Martinique & Breton, who had flair, saw that first stapled magazine & chapbook by Aimé Césaire & knew that that was the future of French poetry.

3. But I'm getting away from the Maghreb. It is important to restate the outrageous neglect, or rather the willful distortion, of Maghrebian &, by extension, Arabic poetics & their influence. The French anthropologist, Germaine Tillion, had a wonderful expression to describe the links of the Mediterranean; she called one of her books *Les Cousins de la Mediterranée*, (translated as *The Republic of Cousins*) & showed how any citizen of the Mediterranean periplos, from the Straights of Gibraltar to the Turkish coasts via El D'Jezair or Mallorca & Marseilles, the Greek Islands & the Gulf of Tripoli, had more in common with each other than with any man or women more than 200 miles inland – north or south of there.

4. Ezra Pound had gotten a whiff of that possibility via Bérard's take on *The Odyssey* as possibly a Phoenician sailing manual for the Mediterranean – thus Homer not only as first epic poet of the so-called "western tradition" but also, & maybe primarily so if you value *The Odyssey* higher than the tiresome male macho war mongering of *The Iliad*, as a highly skilled technical translator. But Pound missed it elsewhere, i.e. among the troubadours. To his excuse it must be said that he was not the first & last one to do so, and that it was easy to miss it there, given that romance philology had always done its best to hide or negate any links with the south.

5. As Maria Rosa Menocal recounted the story in a recent book, the field of romance philology has done everything in its power to negate an Arab origin or even strong originary influence on what it perceived as the origin of European lyric. Open your American Heritage dictionary & the etymological root for the word troubadour will be giving as a reconstructed, presumed & unattested (i.e. marked with a *) Latin root "tropare." And yet it has been known since at least 1928 (through the work of Julián Ribera), that the obvious root is the Arabic word "taraba" "to sing," and specifically to sing poetry; tarab means song. Pound too was looking for a euro-origin of lyric poetry, and in his 1913 essay on the Troubadours he concedes a vague possibility – as far as the tunes of their canzos are concerned: "They are perhaps a little oriental in feeling, and it is likely that the spirit of Sufism is not wholly absent from their content." And in the essay on Arnaut Daniel he writes: "And he may, in the ending 'piula,' have had in mind some sort of Arabic singing, for he knew well letters, in Langue d'Oc and in Latin.... So it is like as not he knew Arabic music, and perhaps had heard, if he understood not the meaning, some song in rough Saxon letters." And that's it; once Pound has established the origins of Euro-poetry in the canzone, it's transformation & perfection by Dante, he is ready to move to China & Japan. Clarity was to be found only in the North, either the Asian one, or the Mediterranean one, the Mediterranean south dismissed in one 1932 footnote from *Spirit of Romance*: "1932: Spanish point of honor, romanticism of 1830, *Crime passionel,* down to sardou and the '90s, all date from the barbarian invasion, African and oriental inflow on Mediterranean clarity."

6. Blackburn, as far as I am aware, followed Pound & didn't look further south – though he lived in Al-Andalus for awhile. Besides his lovely mid-century reworkings of the troubadour treasure trove, he also translated *The Cantar de mio Cid*, the *Poem of the Cid* – ironically the name itself comes from the Arabic Sayyidi and means "My Lord," though the heroics of the poem consist in the Cid's fierce battles against the "Moors" – the Arab-Berber civilization of Al-Andalus – which in the medieval Spanish mind need to be exterminated from Spain.

7. Jacques Roubaud, great *Oulipian* & connoisseur of Proensa, however also remains in the main stuck on the northern latitudes: talking of the canzone, the invention of a new form & the play & joy of rimes this allows, he mentions, along with he troubadours, "les trouvères français, troubadours portugais, poètes siciliens et italiens jusqu'à Dante et Pétrarche" and their echos in the German Minnesänger – but no Arab sources. When explaining the kind of love *l'amour courtois* was, he does brings in the concept of "al Ishk," love as malady towards death, but that's all.

8. Thus a refusal, century-long, to connect the Mediterranean, to open up to the Arabic. An entry, I think, maybe possible now via the work – in French – of young post-independence Maghrebian writers. Their French is new, crisp, meztico'ed, a "langue or littérature mineure" (as Gilles Deleuze and Félix Guattari propose in relation to Franz Kafka). And through them maybe we can then look back up north, toward the countries of Pound & Mallarmé. Sitting in the weirdly named "Hôtel Transatlantique" (a colonial French hotel chain) in El Oued, the "Village of a Thousand Domes," an oasis of the Souf in the North-eastern corner of the Algerian Algeria, in 1977, having just received Abdelwahab Meddeb's first book, *Talismano* from his publisher Christian Bourgois in Paris: an incredible 30 page opening description of wandering in the medina of Tunis is followed – *instanter*, no cut, not even the seam of collage, but as rhizomatic offshoot – by a picnic in Venice on the tomb of Pound.

9. And Meddeb is not the only one. Let me mention just one other major Maghrebian figure, the Algerian poet Habib Tengour. Core to his quest is the ongoing invention of a Maghrebian space for and of writing, the ongoing quest for the identification of such a space and self. For, as another Maghrebian, Jacques Derrida put it: "Autobiographical anamnesis presupposes identification. And precisely not identity. No, an identity is never given, received or attained; only the interminable and indefinitely phantasmatic process of identification endures." Or, Tengour in a kind of manifesto piece, "Maghrebian Surrealism," that situates the tradition of French Surrealism as a late local variation of a much older and wider practice:

Who is this Maghrebian? How to define him?

"The woods are white or black despite the hidden presence of nuances. Today definition fascinates because of its implications. A domain that misleads. Political jealousy far from the exploded sense of the real.

Indeed there exists a divided space called the Maghreb but the Maghrebian is always elsewhere. And that's where he makes himself come true.

> *Jugurtha lacked money to buy Rome.*
> *Tariq gave his name to a Spanish mountain.*
> *Ibn Khaldûn found himself obliged to give his steed to Tamerlaine.*
> *Abd El Krim corresponded with the Third International....*

The core achievement of his poetics is thus the successful relay between modernist Euro-American experiments and local traditions of sociopolitical and spiritual narrative explorations: "It is, finally, in Maghrebian Sufism that surrealist subversion inserts itself: 'pure psychic automatism,' '*amour fou*,' revolt, unexpected encounters, etc.... There always resides a spark of un(?) conscious Sufism in those Maghrebian writers who are not simply smart operators – go reread Kateb or Khair-Eddine."

10. And many others – some translated, some, no, many, untranslated and in dire need of translation – both for their poetry and narratives, but also for their thinking about the multicultural ("MultiKulti" as they say in Berlin) & the bi- & multilingual. Here, to close, a quote by the Moroccon writer Abdelkebir Khatibi, who has a whole book – *Love in Two Languages* – that reflects on these questions, brining in Arabic, that other, older language of the Maghreb, from which even less has been translated so far:

> Yes, I spoke, I grew up around the Only One and the Name, and the Book of my invisible god should have ended within me. Extravagant second thought which stays with me always. The idea imposes itself as I write it: every language should be bi-lingual! The asymmetry of body and language, of speech and writing – at the threshold of the untranslatable. (Abdelkebir Khatibi, *Love in Two Languages*, p. 5)

Which leads him to say in another essay that what would indeed be extraordinary would be to write "à plusieurs mains, à plusieurs langues dans un texte qui ne soit qu'une perpétuelle traduction" – to write with/in several languages a text that would be but a perpetual translation.

11. Well, no, I haven't closed yet, & don't want to – rather I would like to end by opening this discussion up even further, responding to a need visible / audible now more than ever in the Maghreb, to move even beyond those two languages, French & Arabic, which are both colonial impositions even if there lies close to a millennium between their visitations upon the lands of the Maghreb, and to open up to the autochthonous Maghrebian tongues, the various Berber languages. "Il y a du pain sur la planche," there's "bread on the board" as an (untranslatable) French saying has it – meaning there is much work ahead for the translators, and exhilarating work it is, deep down in the salt mines of all our languages.

The Adverse Language

YVES DI MANNO

A language is never alone. Rather, it remains in constant dialogue with other, contiguous languages in both space and time. Perhaps even more than prose, poetry is generally written in the background or in remorse of *other texts,* supremely executing the models (foreign or otherwise) on which it rests so as to foment its heresies and internal revolutions.

One might consider (as I certainly do) the opening of poetic frontiers in the last thirty years of the 20th century to be one of the major events in our literary history, given the lingering effects of its fallout on the whole of our production. To the point that we will probably see this phenomenon as a decisive criteria (or an exemplary reading grid) when the time comes to more or less objectively assess the final results of the period in question.

We're not there yet, and many a brushstroke must still be added before this fresco will be complete. Let us at least recall certain facts.

Beginning in the 1960s, then in the course of the following decade, a new generation of writers struggled to break the strange isolation of our country – poetically speaking – with respect to the majority of great foreign languages, by translating (often for the first time) a growing number of foreign poets, whether immediate predecessors or major contemporaries. Many of them inscribe this work in the margins of their "own writing," in order to find a new approach to questions concerning the deficiencies of "free verse," and more generally of everything that had been suspended in our own tradition, once traditional metrics were abandoned. Cutting a path into these quasi-virgin lands and confronting works that would not fail to have an effect on their own writing, these poets rushed to transform the French landscape, opening to the whole of contemporary poetry an era of turbulence, lightning flashes, and fertile imbalances.

This is an allusion – among so many others – to the *step forward* taken by Denis Roche when he brought Ezra Pound into the French kerfuffle, in tandem with his own rowdy work. To the groundbreaking work done by *Action Poétique*, around Jacques Roubaud, for the rereading/rewriting of the European avant-gardes, as well as of more distant legacies. To the gesture of Michel Deguy, placing his *Revue de Poésie* (from 1977 on *Po&sie*) under the sign of the polyphony of languages and plural translation. To the efforts of Jean-Pierre Faye to commingle the "movement of the change of forms" with an international set. To those of Claude Esteban through his "parallel" poems, of Emmanuel Hocquard who applied his Objectivist detergent to lyric poetry, and of many magazines – *Argile*, *In'Hui*, *Banana Split* – each working in its own way toward a common goal. In a word, to all this broad, collective journey during which French poetry attempted, for two full centuries, to redefine its rules and invent, from a decidedly formal perspective, a *second Modernity*.

As we know, this activity did not produce the desired results. Nor was it a total failure, far from it: particularly in editorial terms, the presence of foreign poetries in literary journals was significantly increased, and many seminal works – as well as other, lesser known titles – have been translated into French. This movement has continued to the present day, and direct encounters between poets of all nationalities have become more common thanks to events like the Biennale du Var-de-Marne and the translation seminars at the Foundation Royaumont, for example.

But the underlying principle of this leap toward *the other* and *elsewhere*, which tended to trouble the secular habits (as well as the most secret laws) of French poetry through the practice of translation by forcing a confrontation with the foreign *from the inside*, seems to have fallen through and evaporated in the aethers, not without leaving – we can see them occasionally – beautiful sulfurous trails of smoke hanging in the sky.

It would require some effort to determine why the French poem has hardly been effected by this phenomenon. Why has the rapid intrusion of foreign bodies into our language not resulted – or only marginally so – in a redefinition, indeed a veritable recasting of French verse, since it revealed to us hitherto unseen perspectives, especially with respect to prosody?

For parallel to the redefinition, the redeployment of writing, that was where the translator was heading, at least in the case of those poets I have just mentioned. They all harbored (you can't have one without the other) their generation's great suspicion of "visionary," oracular, *inspired* writing. Now, the act of writing through the voice of another writer *while wearing the yoke* of one's own language – a language now outdistanced and suddenly foreign – was inevitably instrumental in the conquest of other literary spheres, via its tendency to materialist and modern estrangement.

We must admit that this perspective has curiously diminished of late, and that we currently stand at the antipodes of a project that bore its share of Utopia, yet had the great merit of envisioning the rift represented by translation as implicitly inscribed in all poetic practice from a *concrete* angle – whether syntactical and metrical – rather than insisting on emotional states or the private life of so-called "authors."

What can we say about the last twenty years with respect to this project?

On the one hand (and of course this accompanies a striking formal regression in poetic writing itself) a return to the use and the "classic" finality of translation: that is, of a chiefly *documentary* conception of transferring a text from one language to another. Whereas the transposition of the foreign poem should also allow the creation of a latent grammar, a syntax or "rhyme" unknown in our language, and working at its metamorphosis, its decentering, its new beginnings.

On the other hand (in the ranks of the last modern battalions), a hasty recycling of earlier works, a normalization of the written word (as of language here), and a superficial formalism to the detriment of the density, the materiality of the poem (and of its prosodic structures) – without revealing a real desire to broaden its scope to other spheres of discovery.

In a word, with very few exceptions, a loss of affection takes over.

For we must come to the following conclusion: unlike their immediate predecessors, those poets having emerged these last few years seem only marginally concerned by what is happening outside of their immediate circle – however limited it may be – and are obviously not looking to open any new frontiers. They care little for translation, only rarely quote from foreign authors (aside from a few obligatory references: Stein or Celan, according to the clan...) and hardly seem to perceive what is at stake in this exchange between languages, when it comes to writing. No more than they claim any real filiation, beyond two or three "big brothers," whom they look upon obligingly.

If it were true (though perhaps it is merely a sign of confusion in these heady times), this tendency would signal a major break with the work of the two preceding generations, both in France and abroad, and would in my opinion indicate a stagnation, if not a more harmful regression.

For we have in no way exhausted the various registers of those foreign voices that ultimately transformed French poetry. Nor have we seen a decline in those songs that altered it, bearing as they did the distant sounds in which the *rift* was glimpsed by all those who attempted, in confronting words come from without, to break through the boundaries of their own language.

It would be regrettable if, abandoning a practice of translation that is both experimental and applied, poets wound up turning away from this dual mode to writing against the grain, and in spite of themselves; or if they renounce exploring the various prosodic roads that open to them, along the "path of forgetting": for *the test of the foreign* (to use a felicitous phrase) would lead them to cross otherwise unknowable thresholds. And to bring to light, by this very confrontation, otherwise constellated unpublished pages on which the modern poem is endlessly felt and written in the mirror of an *adverse language* lying just beneath the surface of their own.

Deciphering *coming towards*
an invisible alphabet.

○ *Translated by Guy Bennett*

Remarks on Translating & (Re)Source

JULIETTE VALÉRY

*Has there been an evolution in the relationship between source texts and target texts?**

What bothers me in the notion of "evolution" is the underlying notion of progress. It seems to me that there have been a series or sequence of shifts and transformations, though not necessarily in the same direction. As a text takes shape it gradually becomes independent from its "source." I'm also bothered by the idea of "target." In the dictionary I find that "source" and "target" are terms used in automated translation, that is, translations done by machines. I would be curious to see a poem translated by one of the programs companies use to translate the users' manuals of the machines they manufacture. Well, maybe not – just the thought of it strikes me as lacking in interest. That said, the terms *texte de départ* and *texte d'arrivée*, which are sometimes used in the context of literary translation, are not satisfactory either. For me (for us) what happens in between the two is where translation is played out. And this obviously implies the acceptance of a loss or disappropriation, indeed, an fundamental destruction: the text loses the very substance it is made of; the translator becomes a *passeur* of someone else's words and runs the risk of being mistaken or "betraying." Yet he signs a new text, a text he has written (reappropriation), a text he reveals in a new light. Like a technician he examined it, then copied it out in his own language, which the text in turn makes strange. As Norma Cole

* The italicized questions were those distributed to panelists as issues to consider in their talks.

has written: "Taking words from someone's mouth when the text requires something about the independent necessity of facts." (from *Mars*)

How can we define the notion of an "original text" in translation? Can we imagine a translation without a source text?

That's called writing, but isn't writing also translating, say from the *lingua franca* into one's own language? In my opinion every translation becomes an "original" text. That's why we (Un bureau sur l'Atlantique) defend our choice of never publishing the original text opposite the French text, which must stand alone on the page and exist in its own language, with neither crutches nor bodyguards.

What is the nature of collaboration in translation?

It is fundamental, and present every step of the way, whether you're translating as a group or not, or working with the author or not. To translate is to accept to be many, a sentence without a subject, like Norma Cole's sentence above. An unending montage of reading and writing, a *mise en echo* not unlike a *mise en abyme*. The translator becomes a spectator, an observer in a little theater to which he invites a text. An enigma to unfold or a grammatical inquiry, to paraphrase Emmanuel Hocquard. Obviously an actor and an author, too, and that doesn't mean working alone.

Has the relationship between French and English transformed over time?

That's not for me to say.

◦ *Translated by Guy Bennett*

Poetry

GUY BENNETT

MICHEL BULTEAU

YVES DI MANNO

STACY DORIS

JEAN-MICHEL ESPITALLIER

CHRISTOPHE FIAT

ERIC GIRAUD

JOSEPH GUGLIELMI

BENJAMIN HOLLANDER

PIERRE JORIS

JENNIFER MOXLEY

DOUGLAS MESSERLI

COLE SWENSEN

PAUL VANGELISTI

Saint-Ferréol's Hôtel (*Chambre Gauguin*)

deep this blue
square its double
door dream shield
sharp
effective locks
out noise heat
licks docks in
distance unseen through
the twice
thick windows 8:05
AM 20
o

Le Jardin des Vestiges

is
where now it
was then the broken
stone park
palimpsest
superposes time
on language hemmed
sidewalks fence
the mall market Greek
film Fuji green Roman
Kodak gold

Rue du Petit Puits

400
wells drilled I'm
told the Panier
one
by one filled
with time as he
says
people of
a night walk chill
once bar after
bar fell in

Ferry Boat (*Intérieur*)

how deep this
water when first
they came
from Phocaea sailed to
this bright port what
their thoughts
what skies
the life behind
they left
for
this rich
blue

Quai du Port (*d'après Flaubert*)

a
blond hair black
beard white skin
blue vein olive
tint bright eye
dark gaze cloak
cloth suit sheet
robe vest
turban collar
hundred tongue
Babel

Chez Basso (*d'après Benjamin*)

the table
of eternity luminous
this
illusion wine
marvels my
solitude shadows
to prism
the flower form
identical blue
silk intensity
a
curious love
this my state

Four clouds whose wood cracks
Thwart the flames. Lost in the wrong note
Of the macadam, eyes become
Vowels. The crumpled paper barks.
At dusk the sinner
With her scarf-like arm contemplates the rhinoceros
Descending the Rhine. Images are wood-
Heaps you wear around your neck.

I've been crushed by a giant hand
I was mistaken for a fly
The night is cold
And smells a little like blood
The ground slopes away
I seem to be slipping
Pity if it's just to get away from insanity

I've seen hundreds of hands
In my faceted eyes
Slap down my anger
You can't always put up with
The dull mind of the satisfied

For the time being
They are stronger
They will always be stronger
We have not understood
That minds must unite
Minds not automatic bodies

Unite and march against
Those who speak to you
In a language contaminated
By their social status

I still have the smarts
I know how to fight
The forgers
But at the first breeze
I'm gone

◦ *Translated by Guy Bennett*

In memoriam George Oppen

I

that which is drawn
in us and strikes
us

this path
seeking itself

(the arch key under
the nave the key

of the hour)
this chant

for the present
where our hands trace their slow
and laborious path

the voice where our voices
are found and name

their sole shining

2

if facing the cipher
ringing the hour
a man walks

and strikes
in us

(on the smooth road)

the crossroads (the milestone)
where our hands stopped

on the clock face

knew again
to draw

a mine

8

it was doors
and hedges (the cell

of glass) it was
words

in the
silent secret

of their light and man

in his peaceless dream
opening the door

on the word (where he

wandered peaceless) whose

mute trace
covered his skin

10

and saw again (one day

of misfortune)

in the twist
of the word

    a word

said not a word

didn't know to devour
on the foreign earth

the man nor the first letter
of his new

language

12

it was
infernos it was

cities
that they knew one after

the other devastate

and when drawn
came

on the deserted plain

a man in the evening

rose again on the sky
the curve of

his scythe

◦ *Translated by Geneva Chao*

In human nature, there's no earth without justice. Anyone's consecration Or confidence even makes the world an emblem, beyond response thus. Sown to an image, somebody executes and expires in longing. Numbs. Whatever wrests or saves life from a vow's deception. Devotion empties, Filters through feeling to what's harder than that; rapt beyond sensing, Engrossed. Drowned in adoring, sacrifices for impression's sake, a gravity, Appearance of dwell or own. Printed or not, each picture is votive, an Invocation, voiced, voted into; an office. Extensible in folding, applicable If practiced, hollow. Thus crystalline: a bell. So sounds.

In an ideal entity, melody's variousness. An idol, toyed with, so ravished From living, rapt, violated, thus wholly inviolate, void, set off where Evisceration's tacitly vaunted, pitting duplicity. Where "cell" names "Share," walls feel soluble but work as windows, igneous, glazed from pain, Impervious to incursion. Form means trust, where anyone fails. Transferred To somebody from a stone, love exceeds its targets by diminishing them. Granite's what gathers: a galaxy, consulting, so conjugal where senses Cohabit. Aside or beside, a blurring at best, contact animates its own Delusions, magnetic, a lens; so where can color exceed spectra? In swiftness Perhaps, ghosted or investment, so speculative if perfidy reverses, and Yearning overtakes its effigy; diversifies.

Gambit means phantom, aftertaste and limb, a flexion so diffracted. Light Implies cell death, programmed, most inherent, a mica, isinglass where fish Adheres, so liquid does. Seed's also glue, an among, so flourishing, virulent. Compensates for touch by directionlessness. Collagen, any skin sticks; Its protection stops transmission in its tracks. Transferred by absorbing, Passed on. Sight fixes so when anyone's recognized, she's put in place, A locus, possibly kissed, craving and nourished, abstracted thus present, Featured even. To perceive's an adherence. Then going on's a hugging Where somebody's held, as with a body of water, feels moving but's Propelled. Though differently in water, gravity holds anyone together and slaps her, Every point whipping into shape. She's almost a synonym of weight, run by Pressure, a cycle which thickens and sinks to dissolution. In or by current, Anyone's a path, mineral so sifting away from herself, compelled to crystal, Refined, gleaned or harvested. A sea illustrates injury's buoyancy, though Hurt must too be bound by atmosphere. Attraction patterns every wave's Ribbon, so locks all sights to a ground. Measure decorates at best, festoons Enjoyment in parcels.

Anyone sees in and because of division. Looking, she cordons. Views veil. So perception damps, but that from which it protects may be brilliant, The blindness of extreme gathering, so unleashed. Cliffs cloak earth. As every Caress, bluffs promise envelopment, insidious then. Skin hides a different Exchange, occludes, so nobody quickens to its coils. Love names blood, A circulatory surge, pumps to the choking of nerves, numbed in excesses. Where anyone's chance is to become what's imagined, sink to the down Of somebody's requisition. Time is its waste. Any emotion that's not a ray Is artifice. Mimics a surge as the one way of proceeding. Duration imitates Undulance in memory, so human minds have uses. In a berry or a dog, Recollection's clean movement, but in anyone presents souvenirs. Term's A smokescreen; décor. What words revere, in tense, is this custom.

If lasting is feared or venerated, it is kissed, adored, so molded to anyone's Picturing. She's willful enough to install it. Somebody's a profusion and Fragility; founds truth in explanation then, ranking surfaces. Expounds By a form of growth, looming into temporary shape; abates. Defies touch As a component of use, so that contact becomes speech, more encompassing Thus. A layer.

So then, to write a book about war? To fabricate a book with some war? But why put some war there where there isn't any (first question!)? And what can I make with war? To describe it (but from what point of view?)? To tell it (based on what experience?)? To denounce it (but according to what ethics?)? As I follow after a good many people (because I follow after a good many wars), the exercise is not without risk (less than that of making war, all the same). The risk of only saying all over again something already-said-already-thought-already-found. Now I contest that, if I am constantly bombarded by real images of real wars, I have never myself made war nor ever seen war up close, which, obviously, is not reason enough to make me hold my peace about the war. And if I have nothing to say, I have to invent it all. For example, a book at war. In its difference from a book about war, the book at war captures some bits of war to make book.

I here begin a new book. That is not a book about the war but a book fabricated with some bits of it.

The Axis of Good

We are the axis of good. We do good and bring good to the evil who do evil to the good. We are the axis of good. We are the axis of good in the fight against evil. Against the axis of evil. The axis of evil does evil where good is found. We are the axis of good in the fight against evil. The axis of evil does evil to the good who fight against evil. We are the forces of good for the good of the forces of good who fight in the end to restore the good of the axis of evil. We are the forces of good. The evil of the axis of evil do evil to the good who are good and we must fight against their good which is evil. They are the axis of evil. We are the axis of good. The axis of evil brings evil to the good who are its evil. The axis of good brings good to the evil who are its evil. The axis of good brings good for the good of the evil who are its evil. We are the forces of good and we must do evil to evil for the good of the axis of evil whose good is evil. We are the axis of good. They are the axis of evil. The good sees that the evil is evil because it is good. Only the axis of evil does evil and wishes evil on the good or does not wish good to what it thinks to be evil and which is good. We are the forces of good in the fight against the forces of evil who wish us evil. We do evil to the forces of the axis of evil for our good because their good is our evil and the good is evil that we do for the good of those who do evil to the good. The good will triumph over the forces of evil. The good will make good triumph. The good will make the good of the forces of good triumph. The good can make good triumph only because it is good. We are the forces of good and we must do evil to the axis of evil. In the name of good. Against the good of the forces of evil. In the name of the good of the forces of good in the fight against the forces of evil. We are the forces of good. They are the forces of evil. We are good and we wish evil to the forces of evil who wish us evil. We are the forces of good and we wish evil to the forces of evil for their good. Though we are bedeviled. The good of the evil is evil. The good of the good is good. The good of the good is evil for the evil. The evil of the good is still good. The good of the axis of evil is always evil. They wish evil to our good which they judge to be evil and which is good. Though we are bedeviled. We are the axis of good. We will wish good to the axis of evil when it has become the axis of good. Though we are bedeviled. The forces of good recognize the axis of evil in that it is evil. The forces of good recognize the evil in that it is not good. The forces of good recognize the evil in that the axis of good wishes it evil. The forces of good are the good insofar as the forces of good can incarnate only good. Though we are bedeviled. The axis of good is the good because the axis of evil wishes it evil. The axis of good will make good triumph over the forces of evil because they are evil and it is the good. Though we are bedeviled.

February–March 2003

○ *Translated by Sherry Brennan*

Batman looks
Like a super hero
And a national hero
Like the others.
All super heroes
Have a sober composition
Especially Batman
The man who is a bat
Because
Batman is of all
The super heroes
The most restless
Because Batman
Does not have superpowers
But only
A super costume
And super accessories
And a super car
Then the truth
Is that Batman
Is first an adventurer
But he is not violent.
American society
Is violent
With the materiality
Of things
And the cinematography
Of existence
And the American flags

Which are abbreviations
Planted
On plantations
Cities
Gas Station
Gravestones
And buildings.
Batman is a stubborn American.
Is it true?
Batman is an abstract American.
Is it true?
Batman is an American who simplifies.
Is it true ?
Batman is an American
Who is
The exact replica
Of Bruce Wayne
Who is another American
Who is the original
Version of a man
Who has a real
American life.

◦ *Translated by Béatrice Mousli*

Documentary of the making the evacuation the solitude the decline the interest rates the torching of real estate the difficulty of possessing anything but furniture the empty fridge the daily patronage of restaurants the bachelor set-up the strength the energy the expense the licenses the booze the limits on what you can buy the specialized shops the dominical restrictions the vestiges of prohibitions the technical school studies the hyperactivity the inventor the politics the borderlines the towns the rivers the vice the strict separation of security and danger the factories turned into rock stadiums the floors the halls the rooms the staircases the terrace vip the skin tight clothing the closet's retort the fuse the eyes the wave the movement the restrained crowd how you force your way through the tightly-packed throng the restrictions on drinking in a certain room the necessity of eating in the sections reserved for this purpose the tension of communities the rancor of blacks the politeness of whites the number of latinos the discretion of asians the business of italians the impetuosity of the irish the rudeness of the gauls *la différence* of the french the by default discretion the silence of distancing the first generations the freeway the return the airports the silos the reservoirs the hangars the railroad tracks the high-speed tracks the raised tracks the standard districts to live in the large two-story buildings the overpasses the grill the chimneys the billboards the cranes the bulldozers the measured parking spaces the streetlamps the entanglements of the freeways and overpasses the busses the semis the gas stations the names of unfamiliar districts the wastelands the gravel the tall grasses nothing to announce nor predict the controlled neglect the trees thinly scattered the reversible climate-control system the advertisements for divorce bankruptcy insolvency done cheap law firms ready to serve you and accompany you through these difficult and painful ordeals the signs for secure long-term storage the quickness with which you excuse yourself at the slightest awkwardness the crowded aisles the carts proportionate width the extreme politeness the signs of education of good citizenship the connectedness of the ads inserted by the listener the reader the spectator the respect for intersections the wait for authorization the difficulty of crossing the cut of advertisements the cut of streets the cut of sidewalks the cut of crosswalks the art of quickly extracting yourself from the meal to return to imperious occupations the hyperactivity even in leisure the low altitude while flying over houses the speckle of above-ground swimming pools surrounding airport zones the noise of jets of monorails of nonstop traffic the parks the controlled anxiety of space the change in bearings the mastery that comes from leaving the street the sudden impression of being an integrated part the visit to banks the kindness of bankers the sympathy the fists the posters the functions the freud figurine the package the pictures of the wife and kids the shirts the dossiers the indications the origin the destination the sojourn the proportionate width of the street / height of buildings the journeys toward production areas the pauses the groundfloors the entryways the facades of buildings the continuity the walk the absence of stopping the direction the exception the intersection the forced pause the wait the white individuals the orange hands the profusion of objects of goods of images of museums the encroachment the progression the grabbing of every place the saturation of the eyes the belief in the heart's rhythm the televisual analogy the publicity saturation the suffocating museums the shrinking of hearts the necessity of pulling out the amplified sound the circulation the grabbing of every place the number of vehicles the incessant activity of the interior of the exterior the impossibility of hearing the current the power of the listener to cut off the one who cuts the control to the vital organs the hundred and five front rooms of the *hôtel château* the apparition of the heads of busts the furtive life of the occupants the talk the apologies the complaints the makers of babies their presumed superiority over the unreproductive the morgue of the unreproductive thanks to the life of the reproductive the reproach of the one for the unfruitfulness of other the absolute equivalence the restored above-ground subway unhealthful the fracas the entanglements the parallels the criss-crossings the distribution the exotic the oil the herb the flowers the wild the tall urban trees the snow the wood the crossbars the necessity of hearing the same thing many times in order to understand it the fulgurant plans of yuppification the targeted urban zones the discreet disappearances the bars the butcher shops the corner stores the arrivals the evictions the novelties the parking lots the residence lots the victorian the contemporary the flourishing of estate planners the areas in the midst of development the forgetfulness the erasure the newness the two-story single-family homes versus the four-story buildings to rent the beneficial depth the standard of square feet the condominiums the investment in communities that were originally cultural the displacements the expansions the luxury the primarily gay neighborhoods the expropriation of communities the moving in of some the moving out of others crime insecurity the center driven toward the periphery the depopulating the neglect the return the reinvestment the polish the gypsies the europeans the vietnamese the chinese the irish the germans the latin-americans the nigerians the african americans the motif the joy the pathology of the couple with their first young child the sharing of tasks the professor the woman lawyer the segments of society the acquiring of buildings of lofts of huge spaces the uninhabited rooms the storage boxes the carpet the meals the delivery services the heat the stains the fingers the vast houses the exorbitant paychecks the references the classical art the unchecked pursuit of sense the discussion techniques of couples the difficulties in passing in speaking the repetitions the cuts

○ *Translated by Jennifer Moxley*

Braque's big round table looks
like a
            dentist's chair
a
nothing to compare it to, *work not life*
blue people
in solid sun
                        light
these
      that turn
blue
from weariness
                        effect   father

and Willendorf Venus looms
echoes of hunting, croo croo and negative hands
shadow level
dim dim of the flash prehistory, taking by street
Holzwege
with
      "reviving the imaginary"

After years of reading research the roots
milky streets
city men proclaim centralism of notes

The plan where I check off the treasure of your hips
and the ray

and
the head pushes from inside: *path* passage that changes name:
playing years and years with panoramic
lies
o city women
near a note that says the *objectivist poet*
George Oppen lived in Toulon

°

Those who believe in transparence right to be wrong
or perish by extremes
when the object wolfs down the subject
exaggerates

°

Newspaper dated Monday May 23
Long, fine legs à la Newton.... Mouth mouth caresses.
In the in the image
Four o'clock. Try to translate "*after dark*".... Slipping, socks
in the dream. Put on for sailor
                    no, kingfisher

°

gustatory sequel, and death pedaling indefinitely
or chain reaction
plus
a geographic leftover
or placing the canal
the cuttlefish's ghost

of those Henri Michaux loved
a whole array, Lautréamont in Namur and Michaux
who looked like Jouvet.

°

going on
to Frank O'Hara
parenthesis: I suspect Michaux jerked off
in front of an aquarium of cuttlefish
and
O'Hara
arrives through a poem of
Beth Raps's, in English from 1993
"Does he wish he'd cast his face?"
and the use of the word "*lid*," couvercle,
paupière the impression of the face
as well as the impression
of a step in *m* in
the sand
each time
impression or molding
not cast
like
the without a trace of literature
and recitative
the rotten of literature

an imprint more or less intense
a kind of kiss
able to go as far as
fornicating

let them call it artificial
running bikes and cherry plums…
O'Hara

our feet cut into the sand

Nos traces dans
                    le sable
and
in
between
your feet
carda
        mon
is
a
body

◦ *Translated by Paul Vangelisti*

I

What he overhears is the underbrush. What he
overhears in translation tears in this underbrush:

lemon grass or cloth, neither lemon grass nor cloth
under that music, or no one under that music by itself.

North of the acacia he points to where she sleeps.
At this age he is told

things like words appear or disappear:
sleep: music: lemon grass or cloth,

three rings of wood make the sound she can't count
and two letters in the bell make the numbers go away.

Once at this age he tells her
to point to where things

like fingers or words
appear to come near her,

and to count in her sleep
the times they disappear.

2

That is the tale which begins
he counts three folded rosebuds

at the mouth of the river.
And these are the words which fill in

milk, palms, the Japanese tongue
this water runs over and shreds in two

for three folded rosebuds
at the mouth of the river.

3

One half will tell it
two times over to the mouth of the river.
One half will tell it
two times over and overhear it
a third at the foot of the mountain.
Their fingers will paint it
in the heart of the forest,
as a heart and a forest,
then those too will disappear with their fingers.

monsoonish .
            on back porch
awaiting dawn through a
curtain of rain. to write
whatever . *quod*
libet all the unwritten
letters to you . and you.
and you. The noise of rain
on the brain. Do not
mention pens. Wet dogs'
bark. Do not mention rain.
A quarter is a small
space, except when it's
empty. Rub Al Khal. Long.
7, Lat. 20? Dry spice
Rub Beefy Rancho
Roll-Ups. American
spirit: organic poison.
I wish I were in
Sa'ana. No news is old
news. A break in the clouds.
No joke. She sleeps through
it. Not the Latin quarter either.
The pont Mirabeau. He
was a strong swimmer. They
say. Which leaves a doubt. Do
you need a doubt? Bridge careful
coffee. This morning. Every
morning. Still or again the

back porch the front porch &
back again a smoked cigarette
now that rain don't mention
it has stopped here
there is no room for no doubt.
Every fact is a
miracle. There can be no doubt.
This is the back porch again 5 a.m.
nicotine it is not a moth it is a bee.
the night bee circles the light.
Tighter, more wound up then
any moth. Bounces off the
oddly honeycomb shaped surface
of the porch light. Goes into
darkness. Now a small
mosquito. Thoughts of stag-
nant water. Here by the Hudson
West Nile disease. Pont
Mirabeau. Drowned in a
poem. Birds & mosquitoes.
All places now contemporaneous in
the body. No room for
contempt. The birth of Mithrias
from homesteads. Mystery of
a postcard A. sent from
Newcastle. Paying tribute
to the dead.
Barry MacSweeney, poet,
friend. A birthing card
cycles between the
three of us, the
wheel of Samsara
wheel of common
wealth &
decay.

Telegrammatica per Franco Beltrametti

"Caro, son qui: ti scrivo
(I write to tell you
per dirti..."
(two or three things
  not bad at all
(all words are borrowed only)
vetri / polvere / rossa
no, I have no Greek theatre in my backyard
"continuazione in (p)rosa"
"a dead poet and one alive"
"una specie"
"can laugh at it all"
(la poesia)
(un matin de neige)
"di filosofia d'azione"
AT THE HEART OF THE WORLD
It's our turn. I think so
"wiederholen
abwandeln
meditieren"
and the world is becoming
far less elegant
"un trapasso
dal sangue al sasso"
desolation/ we will be here no longer/ not
j'emporte avec moi
a book to be called
Blows Against The Mother Tongue
a cura de
(toi & moi)

(così così)
vos images
merci, mon ami,
abrazos,
pierre

West

Being here is hearing being when
the sea sets and wind runs into the house
to hide: everything is red. Blood
someone once said of every dead Indian.
There's no doubt I drink too much.
Here. Being here I'm becoming biblical.
The locust threaten to descend. The fires
of early evening create a kind of cozy
campfire upon which we cremate all
that might have occurred to us. There is no news
that hasn't already happened. Still –
and that is the amazing thing, even in a house
away from sunset – there is a kind of sweetness
in the chill, a jacarandad scent that settles
over head: and we believe even at the edge
of our continent we can push forward more, just
a little bit more, yet
we fortuitously forget
and fall back into the sling
of askewed arms. Shhhh, someone says
pointing a gun at my head, don't move.
I don't. I never will again.

26 June 2002

Three Legs, Triangle

The eve of yesterday discloses
an extract of the church, the park
"where we mounted Pegasus."
Here sudden is perceived as all-motion.
The disorientation derives from pronouncing
the dream in reverse, as if in the infant
dawn I had discovered the juxtaposition
of your contrasts. Veil me the face
who passed by too fast to look into.
You saw, you spoke. But beaten
by the sun I sensed only the spin
of our trajectory – down, down
into the great city's center
in an explosion of
cactus and sulfer.

Night and Day

for Howard

Every night now I shoot the stars
like a soldier in a magic land
where the world has sunk into ash.
In my sleep I see a burning
to light all the cities of the map.
I call your name without knowing.
I call knowledge into me without your arrival,
shoot another and lay down my gun.
I beg the wind, please leave me a breath,
But the years run by in a vacuous rush.

I pray that you will forget me
without regret. But no, in the morning
you sit up. The black tar of daybreak
is cracked by your very yawn.
Shhh, you whisper. There are no stars.
There are no years. The map is trapped
in the trunk of the car. In the rain everything
is green again. And the gun you held
was my arm. Come along, it's time to get up!

13 November 2003

The Lock

after "Le Verrou" by Jean Honoré Fragonard

Is between her crescented neck and the open legs of the bed
where passion pleats the fragile back into a diamond
of cut geometry, two complimentary angles,
one his thinly veiled backside, a fist of arrogant,
devious Eros garroting her round the yellow waist
the other the dread stripped voiceless "o,"
phantom drawn on her grey swept lips,
the vain escaping utterance muffled
in lengths of ceiling to floor red folds
that leave the mind no quarter.

Locked by the practiced sense, our intimate, stubborn,
memories are textured, 'til what resistant fence of spleen
we lastly held is lathed away, roughened by ignorance
but not yet gallant for the love of frank luxury
we might – imbue the satinate room in blood metaphors,
invent an impotence en route to the sensorium,
just as lost when thinking, where pricked
the slight secretion of his quiver? The sweep of tongue
through the peel of fabric, layer upon layer away from her skin?

We are exactly aroused by arrangement,
as the unaccustomed eye in too much light
does redden, weep and shut, around the head
do creep a suite of senses not our own: unlock follows lock
follows contrition swept solitude, tiny bird dead in the scoff
of moonlight, curled desire, and then the triangle of deep light,

followed by the obvious question: must it always
end in shadow, line, brushstroke, etc. What sort of a man
would leave us here, resistance out of reach?

The device is that of an egoist, the scene is left
in three-quarters shade of imagination,
the rotation is one without motion, a beauty pellicle held
far from the limit of subsequence, inconsequent moment
from which rises the master on his toes and draws an "x,"
extends and reaches for the lock, but the sliding bar remains as painted,
forever distant from its staple, and in this shaving of space
our lives are made flightless thought, his skein of threaded
gold-light passing through even the thickest juncture.

Aeolian Harp

for and after John Wilkinson

Ribboning dreams unspool in a discarded heap
of oppressive gravity, remember when life
was still compelling, your talents in truck
for fealty, the luxurious future at hand, pastoral
lack of capital in the vernal fervor couched;
"make something of yourself," for example a man
or a picture of archaic pride atop an old armoire,
"pull yourself up by your bootstraps," as did those
bargained away first sons whose whims were nursed
by sins far worse than sacrifice, remember when
you thought yourself less played upon by circumstance,
little by little by literal evidence you've come to be
misplaced, the time it took to spin these words has
long since disappeared, befooled by work the reading
of which another dreamer will unspool, do take your place
in pushing back the clock, small perks won't allow
a stay of revelation, the fear of ignorance has
become the vested knowledge of stupidity, choice
the slow extinction of your faculty for longing,
and the place you would go back to of an orbit unreal.

The Baroque Garden

In a long history of openings
which begins in the warm
closed gardens of the Middle Ages, where nature began
for the first time, in glass doors, a long
series of outsides, a here after here, necessarily serial
like a body entering a doorway, and spilled over.
                                                            And the body becomes
outside with age; they say the stance,
                              for instance, while standing in line for the bus, basically,
the body flays itself upon the world in slow motion, the garden, quite
        naturally, opens
quite naturally, a leap
                              from all that is safe
                                    we are infinitely made. And now mathematically
arranged as an archipelago – with the proper opera glasses,
                                    they could list every palm, with these equations,
with which we are long.

Le Bosquet des Sources

He saved the trees already in place by carving little waterways no more
than six inches
wide
among
a savings bank for trees. There was a forest he wanted to save

as paths, whose paths

whose canals were often only   he built a garden
of interconnecting water
laced, he

saved trees like others save stamps. Exact. One definition of an island is
that which is
new.
And so the eye is constructed as something not far from an ocean. You
made it
more quiet. Water adds silence
to a forest
in which each tree began alone.

Euclid's 8th Theorem

That identical parallel objects placed a different distances
from the eye are not seen in proportion to their distances
proving the field of vision to be spherical
like trees that, though identical, move at different speeds
and all the paths
that started out infinitely curved
                                        roll slowly
across a space full of birds until the forest slows down so much
that a man can carefully plan
to place the body equidistant,
                                        the body in the middle
which is his
                    will wait
                                    until the power of want ignites the tops
of the trees in a line, one by one, even a whim
will prove the Renaissance wrong:
                                    It is not a plane hung before the painter's eye
like a window, but a float from a Japanese fishing net, red
that made it all the way across the ocean on a single storm
                                                                placing the world
among its objects
                causes a crossroads
which is another mode of locating the body
as a series that necessitates a love of time.

Disappointment came to find us as we were
lighting cigarettes for ghosts, babyface.
The thunder never mentioned who she was.
Facility is a door declined at both ends
as the police like to say: toujours
the moon toujours the moon toujours.
Because usually at that size, my dove,
there's only metabolism and survival.

Trappers and farmers are now about to blur
as the speed of the film reaches a place
of comfort or a suitable just because.
Movies, like a long weekend, sometimes tend
to leave the ordinary a little dour
or at least more interesting or pure
than most things. Movies aren't really like love
but a better way to screen arrivals.

Basically happy days when you're not sure
of anything much except that same space
the brusque white dog or jaunty crow undoes
upon waking as who or how. What lends
to the dazzling vagueness of time is the lure
of repetition, getting it right, surer
than before that one notices just above
the trees a restlessness nothing rivals.

Space, then, while it might look like the cure
mostly arrives a little late to outpace
the sweet birds' twitter and lilt, the buzz
and swell of light heading right to the end
of staring. White, white, blue, purple, green stir
the other side of memory impure
as ear or heart in a dish or slap ungloved.
And ever that clever curse of revival.

As you appear more rigorous and sure,
you become more easily profligate. Erase
how you put your idea to it, what was
clarity meant swinging at least eleven
of those suckers. Enough temperature,
thank you, for elasticity to endure
my silly little thing however much of.
Tomorrow, yesterday, today – archival.

Some prefer enduring it for dancing.
Face it, most want having it commonplace.
Puzzlingly enough, anything sadder
pretends to the economic or comic,
surely a common frustration if
alluringly simple to renounce. Here
love will never find a way just something
to rival its often bang bang start.

A man ordinarily has to lose to err.
Or not. What nobody has the face to.
All are eligible only because
jive is jive no matter the pitch of spending.
Life's thorns gawk like children of the lower
classes. Alas. All are waiting for rain, sure
of that which is habitually beloved.
Rum-tum-tum. Rum-tum-tum. The queasy lull.

What is all this juice and all this joy,
said Hopkins, or was it Truman, or just
another poet trying to act like
a poet on the radio. Languorous
is no moral outside language, even
when you must, at every opportunity,
decline. Eight is what a wheelbarrow does,
eight is what must sound already eaten.

PARTICIPANTS

GUY BENNETT is the author of four collections of poetry, most recently *Drive to Cluster* (2003). His work has appeared in magazines and anthologies in Brazil, Canada, France, Italy, Mexico, Morocco, and the USA. Recent translations include books and chapbooks by Nicole Brossard, Jean-Michel Espitallier, Mostafa Nissabouri, Valère Novarina, and Jacques Roubaud. He is the publisher of Seeing Eye Books, co-editor of Seismicity Editions, and a contributing editor to the *New Review of Literature* (USA) and *Électron Libre* (Morocco). In 2005 he was named Chevalier de l'Ordre des Palmes Académiques by the French Minister of Education. He lives in Los Angeles.

VINCENT BROQUA is one of the founding members of Double Change (www.doublechange.com) and a curator of the Double Change reading series in Paris. He lectures in British and American literature at the University of Paris 12. He was a Fulbright Phd student in 2002.

MICHEL BULTEAU participated, in 1971, in the *Manifeste Électrique*. He is the author of numerous books of poetry & prose, including *Ether-mouth, slit, hypodermique* (1974), *Des siècles de folie dans le calèches étroites* (1976), *Les filles des eaux* (1982, 1997), *Flowers* (1989), *Poèmes 1966– 1974* (1993), *L'effrayeur* (2000), and *Sérénité moyenne (poèmes 1990 – 1996)* (2000).

Born in 1954, YVES DI MANNO is the director of the poetry series Poésie/Flammarion. He has translated many American poets, among them William Carlos Williams, Robert Duncan, George Oppen, Jerome Rothenberg and Ezra Pound. A poet, and at times an essayist, he published numerous books, his latest publications including *Un pré – chemin vers* (2004), *Partitions, champs dévastés* (1995), *Kambuja, stèles de l'empire khmer* (1992).

STACY DORIS's books written in English include *Conference* (2002), *Paramour* (2000), and *Kildare* (1995). Written semi-anonymously in French are *La vie de Chester Steven Wiener écrite par sa femme* (1998), and *Chroniques new-yorkaises* (2000). She has edited a dossier of new American writing in French for Java, and co-edited the following collections of French poetry translated by American poets: with Chet Wiener, *Christophe Tarkos: Ma Langue est Poétique – Selected Work* (2001); with Norma Cole, *Twenty-two New (to North America) French Poets* (1997); with Emmanuel Hocquard, *Violence of the White Page, Contemporary French Poetry in Translation* (1992).

Born in 1957, JEAN-MICHEL ESPITALLIER is the author of four books of poetry, most recently *En guerre* (2004), and editor of an anthology of contemporary French poetry *Pièces détachées* (2000). In 1989 he co-founded the award-winning magazine *Java*, which has just ceased publication after fifteen years of activity. A translation of his *Fantasy bouchère* (*Butcher Fantasy*) is forthcoming from Duration Press, and his *Théorème d'Espitallier* (*Espitallier's Theorem*), translated by Guy Bennett, was published by Seismicity Editions in Spring 2005.

Born in 1966, CHRISTOPHE FIAT lives in Paris, where, after a brief career teaching philosophy, he now devotes his time to poetry and performance. His latest publications include *New York 2001, Poésie au galop* (2002), *Ritournelle, une anti théorie* (2002) *Bienvenus à Sexpol* (2003) *Qui veut la peau de Harry ?* (2004) and *Epopée, une aventure de Batman à Gotham City* (2004).

Born in 1966, ERIC GIRAUD lives and works in Marseilles. With Holly Dye he has translated a number of American poets, among them Charles Olson, Charles Reznikoff, Stacy Doris, Barbara Guest, Juliana Sphar, Lee Ann Brown, and Peter Gizzi. He co-edited the magazine *Issue*, which just ceased publication after five issues. He is "sub-editor" of the magazine *CCP*, and editor of la collection Américaine of the publisher Le Bleu du Ciel. His work has appeared in magazines in France (*If, Action Poétique*, ...) and in the USA (*The Germ, Fence*). Recent publications include *Des Tâches et des Instruments*, published by Le Bleu du Ciel; *Anthologie, Autres Territoires*, Farrago; *Marcel en Eté*, published by Harpo, *Quitte ou Double*, translation of Raymond Federman's *Double or Nothing*.

JOSEPH GUGLIELMI is the author of more than ten books of poetry and essays. *Aube* (1968) was translated as *Dawn* by Rosmarie Waldrop,), and his latest publications include *Travelogue*, (2000), *Le Pyromène*, (2004), and *Faut suivre* (2005) He has translated into French works by Norma Cole, Cid Corman, Clark Coolidge, Larry Eigner, Rosmarie Waldrop, as well as Jack Spicer's *Billy the Kid*.

BENJAMIN HOLLANDER was born in Israel and emigrated to New York City in 1958, at the age of six. He has lived in San Francisco since 1978. A poet and essayist, his books include *Vigilance* (2004), *Rituals of Truce and the Other Israeli* (2004), *Levinas and the Police, Part 1* (2001), *The Book Of Who Are Was* (1997), *How to Read, too* (1992), and, as editor, *Translating Tradition: Paul Celan in France* (1988).

PIERRE JORIS's most recent publications include *Poasis: Selected Poems 1986–1999, A Nomadic Poetics* (*essays*) and *4x1* (*translations of Rilke, Tzara, Duprey & Tengour*). He has translated Celan, Blanchot, Jabès, Meddeb, Schwitters and others and has received several PEN awards for translation. With Jerome Rothenberg he edited the *Poems for the Millennium* anthologies. He is professor in the Department of English at SUNY-Albany.

Born in 1947, DOUGLAS MESSERLI is the author of ten books of poetry, in addition to works of fiction and theater. For several years is was a professor of literature at Temple University, but left his position to direct Sun & Moon Press. In 1997 Messerli founded a second literary press, Green Integer, which has now taken over most of the Sun & Moon Press activities. Messerli teaches occasional courses at several Los Angeles colleges and universities, most notably at Otis College of Art + Design. He recently received the Chevalier des arts & lettres from the French government for his numerous publications of French literature.

BÉATRICE MOUSLI teaches at the University of Southern California, and is the author of many essays and biographies. Her publications include : *Valery Larbaud* (Grand Prix de la Biographie de l'Académie française, 1998) *Virginia Woolf* (2001), *Les Editions du Sagittaire 1919 – 1979* (2003) and *Max Jacob* (2005).

JENNIFER MOXLEY is the author of *Often Capital* (2004), *The Sense Record* (2002), *Imagination Verses* (1996) and several chapbooks, including *Enlightenment Evidence* (1996), which was translated into French as *Evidence des Lumières* at the Fondation Royaumont in 1998. She lives in Orono, Maine and works as an Assistant Professor of Creative Writing at the University of Maine.

COLE SWENSEN's most recent book is *Goest* (2004); another, *The Book of a Hundred Hands*, will be out from University of Iowa Press in 2005. Her work has been awarded a Pushcart Prize, an Iowa Poetry Prize, a New American Writing Award, and a National Poetry Series. She translates contemporary French poetry, fiction, and art criticism; her translation of Jean Frémon's novel *The Island of the Dead* won the 2004 PEN award in literary translation. Other recent translations include Olivier Cadiot's *Future, Former, Fugitive* and Pierre Alferi's *Oxo*.

JULIETTE VALÉRY, is an artist and a translator. She co-directs the association Un Bureau sur l'Atlantique and has created in 1993 Format Américain, a series that publishes new translations of contemporary American poetry in a chapbook format. She has herself translated among others Norma Cole, Robert Creeley, Ray DiPalma, Stacy Doris, Benjamin Hollander, Bill Luoma, Bernadette Mayer, Laura Moriarty, Bob Perelman, Cole Swensen. John Taggart, Rosmarie & Keith Waldrop, and Elisabeth Willis. In collaboration with Emmanuel Hocquart, she wrote *Le Commanditaire* (1993), *Allo, Freddy ?* (1996), *L'année du goujon* (1996).

PAUL VANGELISTI is the author of some twenty books of poetry, as well as being a noted translator from Italian. From 1971–1982 he was co-editor of the award-winning literary magazine *Invisible City* and, from 1993–2002, the editor of *Ribot*, the annual publication of the College of Neglected Science. In 1981 he received a Translators Fellowship from the National Endowment for the Arts, and in 1988 a Poetry Fellowship from the same Endowment. In 2001, his *Embarrassment of Survival: Selected Poems, 1970–2000,* appeared from Marsilio/Agincourt in New York. Currently, with Luigi Ballerini, he is editing a five volume anthology of American poetry from 1960 to the present, *La Nuova poesia americana,* for Arnoldo Mondadori in Milan. Vangelisti is the founding chair of the Graduate Writing program at Otis College of Art + Design.